The Dominican Experiment

A Teacher and His Students Explore a Garbage Dump, a Sweatshop, and Vodou

Michael D'Amato
and
George Santos

iUniverse

THE DOMINICAN EXPERIMENT
A TEACHER AND HIS STUDENTS EXPLORE A
GARBAGE DUMP, A SWEATSHOP, AND VODOU

Copyright © 2014 Michael D'Amato and George Santos.

All rights reserved. No part of this book may be used or reproduced by any means, graphic, electronic, or mechanical, including photocopying, recording, taping or by any information storage retrieval system without the written permission of the author except in the case of brief quotations embodied in critical articles and reviews.

iUniverse books may be ordered through booksellers or by contacting:

iUniverse
1663 Liberty Drive
Bloomington, IN 47403
www.iuniverse.com
1-800-Authors (1-800-288-4677)

Because of the dynamic nature of the Internet, any web addresses or links contained in this book may have changed since publication and may no longer be valid. The views expressed in this work are solely those of the author and do not necessarily reflect the views of the publisher, and the publisher hereby disclaims any responsibility for them.

Any people depicted in stock imagery provided by Thinkstock are models, and such images are being used for illustrative purposes only.
Certain stock imagery © Thinkstock.

ISBN: 978-1-4917-2600-6 (sc)
ISBN: 978-1-4917-2602-0 (hc)
ISBN: 978-1-4917-2601-3 (e)

Print information available on the last page.

iUniverse rev. date: 3/15/2016

Praise for Michael D'Amato's bestselling book, *The Classroom*

"*The Classroom* is full of imaginative, original, and very practical advice for teachers. It is fun to read, and if applied by teachers all over the country it would make classrooms much more interesting and students better educated."

—Howard Zinn, *A People's History of the United States*

"D'Amato challenges educators to teach outside the box and make learning the fun, exciting, and mind-stretching experience for students it ought to be."

—Stacey Slaughter Miller, editor for the *Wall Street Journal*

"Humor and insight are hallmarks of this witty, inspirational book from an experienced urban middle-school teacher . . . (It contains) 180 tips, tricks, and classroom activities that will help you motivate your students to take charge of their own learning."

—*NEA Today Magazine*

"I recommend the reading of this book for all educators who would like to give their classrooms a 180-degree turn with the book's 180 strategies, activities, quotes, etc. Take a few tips from a Teacher of the Year to make your students excited about their learning."

—Anthony Bland, New Jersey Department of Education

Contents

Foreword vii
Preface xiii

Chapter 1   We Can Do So Much More 1
Chapter 2   Any Other Monsters on the Island
             We Should Know About? 12
Chapter 3   Hell on Earth 32
Chapter 4   Education Is Not an Industry; It Is a Right 56
Chapter 5   They Listed *Papi Chulo* as Their
             Number One Life Goal 66
Chapter 6   Those People You Met Aren't My
             Real Parents, and They Beat Me 83
Chapter 7   A Never-Ending Something Special 102
Chapter 8   Did They Just Throw Something at Us? 108
Chapter 9   But I *Am* Black! 116
Chapter 10   With Charity, the Giving Hand Is Still on Top 128

Epilogue 141

Sonia Pierre and Kevin LaMastra

Foreword

Almost ten years have passed since my first visit to the Dominican Republic and the start of our annual social justice tours. As I began my profession as a teacher of ESL (English as a Second Language), I wanted to learn more about the critical global issues that brought students from all over the world to my New Jersey classroom. Behind every student entering my classroom, there often followed a remarkable but tragic story that motivated each to leave behind families and friends in order to begin a new life in the United States. There were Haitian students whose families were caught up in the political violence of a US-backed military coup, Mexican families who had lost their ancestral farm lands through newly imposed global trade agreements, and a Bolivian student who lived in an area where it became illegal to collect rainwater once the community water supply became the privatized property of a transnational corporation.

Sometimes I would have conversations with strangers who, upon learning that I was an ESL teacher, would be eager to discuss their opinions about my immigrant students and their families. They would openly vent their prejudices and hostilities toward a community they knew only in the abstract. Their frustrations, magnified by the misinformation and provocations of vitriolic media, echoed all of the common myths and distortions surrounding immigration.

In their eyes, my ESL students and their families were parasites, here to exploit the generosity and benevolence of the United States. Their comments revealed that they were largely unaware of the history of US intervention around the world and that they lacked a critical understanding of foreign policies that have created tremendous wealth for the United States and Europe, while perpetuating a cycle of poverty, violence, and exploitation elsewhere. Over time the labels on these policies would evolve, moving from the time of slavery through colonialism to present-day globalization; the *master* became the *boss*, but little else changed.

Although at first I knew little about the countries from which my students came, I later learned that my own country played a key role in shaping the destinies of their homelands. US military and economic interests brought about wars of territorial expansion, the imposition of oppressive military regimes, and the installation of "free trade zones" where international trade agreements established a minimum wage of about eighty-three cents per hour for the workers in these so-called developing countries. I began to understand that the demographics of my ESL classroom, and surges in US immigration in general, were a direct result of these actions. Simply stated, they are here because we are there.

As time passed, some of the detrimental effects of globalization (in its current form) began to make their presence felt at home. The local General Motors plant was closed and then physically demolished, making way for a Walmart opening across the street. For every living-wage job that was eliminated, four or five minimum-wage jobs would be created. Unionized assembly line jobs that once provided a middle-class living for local families were now permitted to move beyond borders to the developing world, where they would be performed by workers earning wages so low that many would have to live without electricity or potable water in their homes. This too had had an effect that would be mirrored in classroom demographics, test scores, and the general well-being of the community at large.

A growing xenophobic and anti-immigrant sentiment began to make its presence felt in this economic context, and the situation was further exacerbated by the aftermath of the September 11 terrorist attacks. No Child Left Behind, Race to the Top, and other neoliberal policies masquerading as education reform but designed to dismantle public education created an environment that pitted teacher against student. Standardized test scores were used to designate "failing" schools and "ineffective" teachers, as well as to give license to private corporations to divert public funds toward private profit, resulting in the development of a billion dollar a year testing industry.

Teachers working in impoverished communities with English Language Learners and other struggling students suddenly found that the students who needed them most had become career liabilities. For example, a teacher's compassion for Haitian refugee students arriving in the aftermath of an earthquake might be tempered by the grim contemplation of how their presence would impact test scores, and ultimately threaten the teacher's professional standing and continued employment. Most teachers did not yet realize it, but the same forces of neoliberal globalization (a market-driven philosophy of deregulation, privatization, and the elimination of social services in the name of "reduced government") that created the conditions that compelled their students to migrate, were also behind the encroaching privatization of public education and the increasing marginalization of the teaching profession.

At this point I set out to create a professional development experience that would help teachers develop a critical understanding of global issues that link directly to their classrooms and the lives of their students. Over an eight-day tour, US teachers travel to the Dominican Republic, where they meet with grassroots activists within local communities. Rather than learning from academics or NGOs, the teachers learn about the daily realities of globalization while immersed among the people most affected. Our learning does not take place behind a desk in a classroom but rather within authentic contexts: standing in a sugarcane field talking with stateless migrant workers, eating dinner with Dominican union organizers after a visit to a free trade zone sweatshop, or while attending a mobilization of the Santo Domingo teachers demanding equitable funding for education.

As Paulo Freire, the father of critical pedagogy, reminds us, critical literacy means being able to read both the word and the world. Because many teacher preparation programs teach multiculturalism as a superficial celebration of differences or a path to assimilation, many well-intentioned teachers wind up lacking a critical understanding of poverty, causing them to view their students and families through a deficit lens. Teachers who have never stepped foot outside of the United States before find themselves struggling to make sense of the desperate living conditions we see in the shantytowns. Throughout the course of the eight-day experience, the comments made by some participants show a remarkable evolution of thought—from mystical thinking ("God made this a poor country, but at least He made it beautiful"), through naïve reasoning ("If only we could replace the dominoes in their hands with books"), toward the development of critical understanding (recognizing our global interdependence and seeing the interconnectedness of our struggles).

Through this eight-day immersion experience, participants learn through intense dialogues with local activists and from one another. By the end of the week many are able to recognize the ideological line that connects Columbus to the free trade zone and ultimately connects to their own communities and classrooms. As they begin to understand our interconnectedness with our hosting communities, feelings of sympathy change to feelings of empathy and solidarity.

The book you are about to read traces one such teacher's experiences on a student social justice trip in July 2010, with other tour highlights sprinkled in here and there. Michael D'Amato has participated in all of the Dominican Republic social justice tours since the project began, and has made incalculable contributions and insights every step of the way.

Although each tour lasts just eight days, participants often remark that upon returning home they spend weeks intensely reflecting upon their experiences. This book represents Michael's process of reflection; this is his effort at honoring what has been shared with him, while trying to make sense of all that he has seen. There are no easy answers to the problems that become visible to us through this experience. The project does not promise to make participants experts in global issues, foreign policy, or international relations. The tour instead provides an experience that may complicate the participants' preconceived notions.

Perhaps most significantly, the experience transforms participants into witnesses. For others, the 60 percent of the world's population who exist on less than two dollars a day are just a statistic, but for us, these people now have a face and a name. Ideologues might promote the virtues of free trade and globalization in its current form, but our participating students and teachers can describe to others from firsthand experience what it is like to work in a free trade zone sweatshop, and pass on the stories of struggle that the workers shared with them on their visits.

Often well-meaning people are reluctant to speak out in the face of injustice when they fear that they lack the qualifications or academic grounding to discuss complex economic and social issues. However, these are not purely academic issues; they are also moral issues upon which all of us have the obligation to act. As Howard Zinn said, "You can't be neutral on a moving train." When injustice exists, in our classrooms or in the world at large, and we choose to remain silent, we are not being neutral. We are moving on that train in the direction of injustice.

Kevin LaMastra, www.friendsbeyondborders.net, November 2013

Michael D'Amato with Yenny Perez
and his students at Alta Gracia

Preface

Imagine being a cocoa picker but never getting to enjoy a chocolate bar. Picture yourself working for a posh hotel where staying for just one night costs more than two months' salary. Or having a job in tourism, but never being able to leave your own island. Think for a moment how difficult it must be to watch people come and go, living like royalty in your country for a week or two, and to wonder what their countries are doing differently to afford them these luxuries. Try to imagine your life without showers or toilet bowls.

Consider what it means to be one of an estimated two million stateless people in the Dominican Republic, mostly of Haitian descent, many of whom are part of the one-fifth club: the more than one billion people on our beautiful planet who live on less than a dollar a day. Legally, they do not exist. No birth certificate. No ID. No diplomas. No way to cash a check. No opportunity even to cast a vote in hope of change. I cannot fathom the level of frustration these people must face as they are reminded daily that they are not among the privileged who get reliable access to clean water, electricity, or plumbing.

If you have the opportunity to visit the Dominican Republic, please do not tell the locals that their country was named the second-happiest place on earth, slightly behind Costa Rica, in a poll featured on CNN in 2009. I'm guessing certain "invisible" communities were skipped over in that survey.

They say we all feel the same pain. I disagree. Nor do I believe any longer that the sun shines for all. I don't think I am a cynic—yet. I just choose to live my life without my head in the sand or in the clouds. I prefer to check where things were made before purchasing them. I'm that guy hunting down the "fair trade" symbol whenever I am in a café. Also, I can proudly say that I have never spent a penny at Walmart, because I subscribe wholeheartedly to the notion that "your dollar is your vote."

I'm attracted to the Dominican Republic because I find it to be an ideal microcosm of some of the world's biggest social concerns: disease, education, gender inequality, immigration, poverty, racism, and slavery. While I teach these concepts regularly in the classroom, I am often left wondering how my students would react if we scrutinized the issues outside the school setting, on the front lines where they take place on a daily basis.

Map by Johanna Contreras

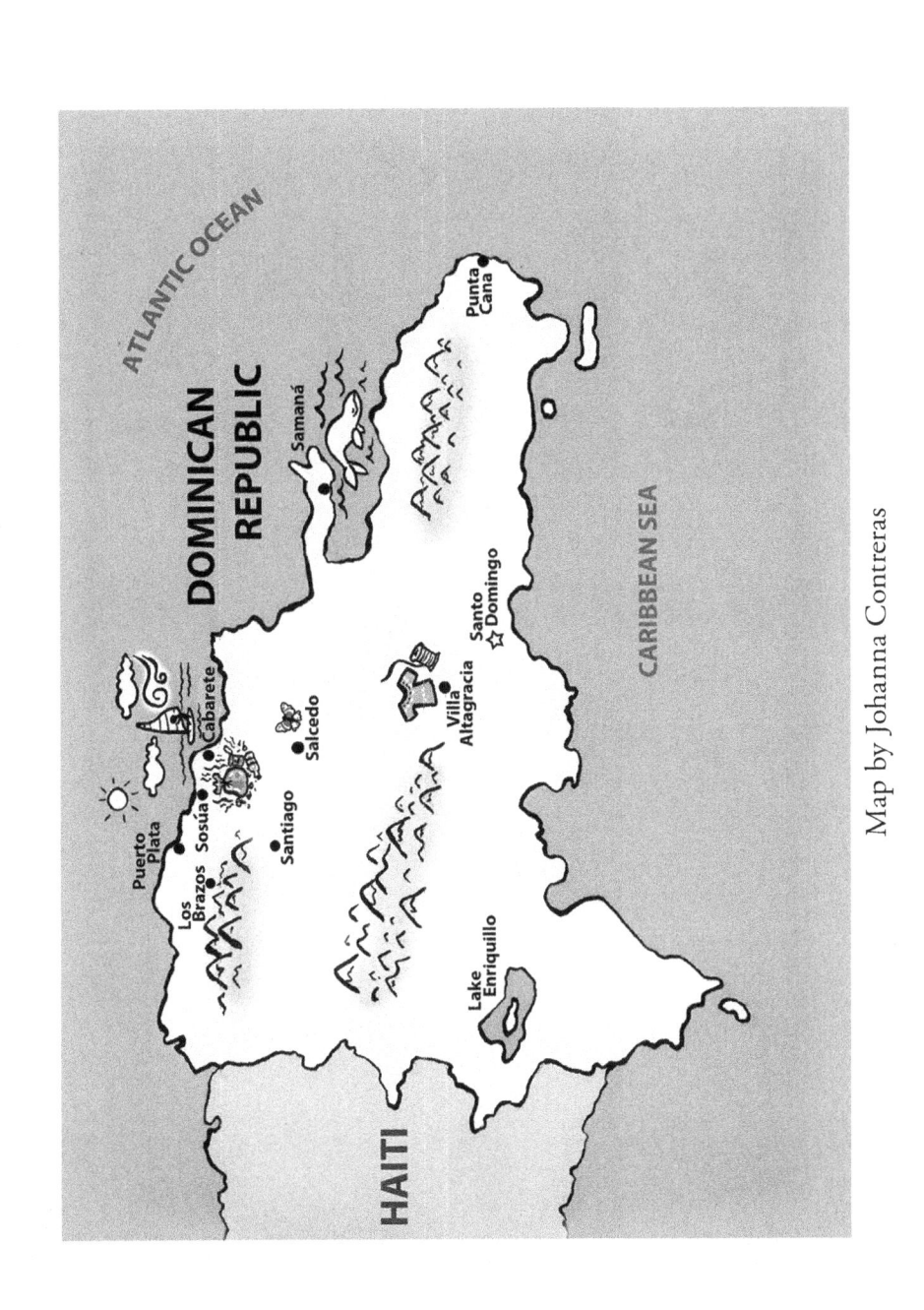

Zobeyda Penaranda, Kevin LaMastra, and Yunior Perez

Chapter 1
WE CAN DO SO MUCH MORE

A buena hambre, no hay pan duro.
(To the very hungry, there is no hard bread.)

"Write down the first three ideas that come to mind when you think about the Dominican Republic" was the Do Now on the chalkboard as my eighth-grade students took their seats, engaging in some last-minute horseplay before class began. When the bell rang, half of them were already busy writing, while the rest were either flipping to a clean page in their notebooks or searching for pens.

One minute into class, I read the Do Now aloud as a subtle prod to the last two distracted students. Since we hadn't discussed the Caribbean much at this point in the year, I asked for a volunteer to share one thought she had so far. A hand went up, but before she spoke, I told the class that I was going to write down my predictions of what their responses would be. (Feel free to play along.) When I finished my short list, I went back to the volunteer, and she shared "white sand beaches" with a proud smile.

When most students appeared done, because they were perusing their current events magazines, I headed back to my lectern and held up my paper with the following terms on it: "tropical paradise," "beautiful Caribbean beaches," "summer vacation." "Please raise your hand if you wrote down any of these words," I said. (You too, reader.) The students took the customary look around the room and, as they saw some vertical movement, more hands slowly rose—nearly 100 percent.

"Okay," I said. "Now, keep your hand up if you had more than one of my words on your list." About half of the hands remained up. My next question revealed my psychology background: "Why do you think I wanted everybody to share their thoughts on the Dominican Republic in this format?"

"Probably to prove us wrong," a student called out with a mischievous grin, and he was quickly rewarded with laughter. After fifteen years of teaching, I have grown comfortable enough to be myself in front of students, so I joined in with a smile.

"No. At least not this time," I said. "Actually, your answers were very accurate. The Dominican Republic, 'the country of endless summer,' is a beautiful tropical paradise with the most pristine beaches I have ever strolled." I gestured to a nearby photo of the country. "With New Jersey being a close second," I said with a grin. "Your answers were remarkable, but as is often said, there are two sides to every story. What do you think I mean by that?"

"I think it means that we have more work to do," another brave student called out.

(It took many years to create a casual climate in my classroom, which has earned the nickname "our sanctuary"—a place where students may express themselves without fear of repercussions from me or their peers. Considering that my longest class is 101 minutes, and considering the stress of a typical teenager's life, class is much more enjoyable and productive when students feel in charge of their own learning and are not forced to work on stale, prefabricated assignments.)[1]

---

[1] At the end of a recent school year, our principal reminded us, "The days of teaching with students sitting quietly at their desks with folded hands are long gone. They need to be challenged and the curriculum palpable." My addition to this maxim is that we should aim for students to look forward to class.

Getting back to the notion that there are two sides to every story, I asked the students for an example. "It's sort of like when you teach about war," one said. "All countries involved are convinced they are the good guys."

Finally, a straight answer. (See, we eventually arrive at our destination. I just prefer to take a more scenic route.) "Excellent connection!" I said. "So, then, why do most people only give romantic descriptions when they first think about the Dominican Republic?"

"The media!" a chorus of students sitting next to one another called out, and I smiled.

"What if I told you that when I think about the DR, as a social studies teacher, the first words that come to my mind are 'poverty,' 'prostitution,' and 'exploitation'?"

A student challenged me. "I thought you don't use the word 'prostitution.'"

"You are absolutely correct," I said. "I have tried to stop using that word after a conversation with my good friend Webster. When I consulted the dictionary, I noticed terms like 'immoral' and 'unworthy' were listed in defining 'prostitute,' which years ago would have been fine, but after meeting with women who are sex workers who educate the new generation on issues from abuse to disease, a shift in my thinking took place. My current classroom stance is to start with the word 'prostitute,' which is the more familiar term, then quickly switch over to 'sex worker,' which, for some, is a tougher phrase."

As the last words fell off my tongue, I suddenly felt that I might have gone too far. But I also thought that, as a teacher who constantly encourages his students to go outside their comfort zones on class assignments, I had to occasionally put myself out there. Of course, the students' gaping jaws were easy to translate: *Mr. D'Amato had meetings with prostitutes?*[2]

The context was this: On my first visit to the Dominican Republic in 2007, on a social justice tour run by my colleague Kevin LaMastra,

---

[2] Surprisingly, such controversial topics never seem to make their way to the powers that be. Maybe it's because teens don't chat with their families about school like in the olden days. Perhaps it's because we have a mutual trust in the classroom. Most likely, it's because they realize that if word gets out, and I am reprimanded, there will be no future stories about their new favorite class topic: sex work.

a man *sin pelos en la lengua* (without hair on the tongue; not scared to speak the truth), we met with a few workers from CEPROSH (Centro de Promoción y Solidaridad Humana, or the Center for Human Promotion and Solidarity) to gain a better understanding of the problems faced by a large number of women on the island, many of them minors. As part of Kevin's prep talk for this meeting, he referred to sex work as a "byproduct of globalization." Admittedly, I was quite skeptical of this particular event on our itinerary, which had us participating in an hour-long discussion led by the organization's program director, a health-care specialist, and a sex worker. My doubts grew when the CEPROSH employees displayed the graphic pages of the comic book *Maritza*, featuring a play-by-play encounter with a customer, and then a detailed flip chart they use to teach young women about the dangers of their profession, similar to what you were forced to watch during high school health class.

The only question I asked during the presentation was about the claim I had heard that, oftentimes, it was the sex workers' own parents who urged the young girls to take to the streets to earn money for the family. The professionals quickly debunked this myth, listing materialism followed by peer pressure as their top motivators. Surprisingly, the speakers made no mention of sex workers choosing the profession to provide a better future for their children. There appears to be a divide between those who believe sex workers choose the work primarily to support their families and others who claim they use that as an excuse to avoid stigma.

The workers reminded us several times during the meeting that sex work is legal under Dominican law, as long as "pimps" or minors are not involved. One bold teacher on our trip, moved by the CEPROSH meeting, actually went into a bordello and came out with photos of the colorful four-page menu the workers use to make it simple for tourists. She referred to it as the "McDonaldization of sex tourism."

During the workers' presentation, we learned that CEPROSH, which is well respected in the community, began in 1989 with three workers and now has more than one hundred serving more than twenty thousand women. All of its funding is international, with USAID being its main supporter. While the group has a medical laboratory at its home site to offer sex workers free STD testing, employees do most of their work at schools, bars, and bordellos, educating the women about disease prevention, discussing the myths versus realities of their occupation, and using role-play negotiations to ensure their safety. Since CEPROSH began its empowerment campaign, it claims the "level of violence against sex workers has significantly gone down." We learned from Sheila Calderon, the program director and outreach coordinator for CEPROSH, that they were able to make an agreement with the Dominican government that all rape cases would be referred to them.

Sheila, a charismatic Dominican looking dapper in her uniform white polo shirt with light blue tie casually knotted, went on to say that CEPROSH's biggest headache right now is that twelve- and thirteen-year-old girls are being pulled into sex work every day by older men who offer them cell phones, new clothes, and trips to the beauty salon. The organization distributes more than one million condoms annually and trains teenagers to work with high-risk peers, using musical acts and guerrilla theater to spread awareness and promote self-esteem.

CEPROSH's other major objective—in addition to the prevention of disease among youths and adolescents, with a focus on family planning—is dealing with HIV/AIDS patients. "It used to be tough to get an HIV test," a worker said. "Now they're free, and information and education are also provided." The worker ended her talk with a statement regarding those who choose to be sex workers: "One thing we're very proud of is that people's consciousness has changed, and their quality of life is constantly improving."

I believe my initial difficulty appreciating the mission of CEPROSH was mostly due to my rigid Catholic school upbringing. But the way Kevin designed the trip, with a thread connecting all of our activities and debriefing sessions making the connections clear, I was able to see that these women are products of their precarious environment—an environment that doesn't offer the plethora of viable opportunities that the United States does. That was the main word that kept resurfacing during our late-night poolside chats, as we tried to wrap our minds around the revelations of each day: "opportunities." The statistic I found most surprising was that sex workers actually have significantly lower rates of HIV/AIDS than do the other women on the island. From there, I was able to see their situations in a new light. The workers at CEPROSH also mentioned that 97 percent of the HIV-positive pregnant women to whom they provide medication go on to deliver healthy babies. I was blown away.

As our class dialogue picked up again, I noticed a few students who were Dominican giving me sour looks. I took the hint. "Before I continue, I feel the need to make a few things extremely clear," I said. "First off, I love the DR and think it is a remarkable country."

A student interrupted. "Then why are you saying so many bad things about us?"

"I see where you are coming from and am so glad you spoke up," I said. "I have had several students in the past make similar comments, and to that question I always reply that if I didn't love your country, I wouldn't have visited it ten times already.

"Taking a step back, you know I am a very critical person. Whether it's grading your papers, discussing politics, or comparing fine restaurants, I enjoy looking at things with a sharp eye. The same holds true when I visit another country. I have friends who are perfectly content sitting in a resort and being pampered for the entire week. I, on the other hand, learned very quickly that I am not the 'all-inclusive' type. During the first and only time I chose to stay at a resort, which cost seventy-five dollars a day for two of us, including all our meals and drinks, I felt totally disoriented and removed from the country. The food was actually quite good, and it was the same beautiful coastline as the beach I prefer a mile away. But one thing was glaringly missing: culture. There was no authenticity to the experience. A friend of mine recently came back from Aruba and said he much preferred his time in the DR because it was grittier. I love that word because it shows a respect for the tough stuff."

The students seemed to find my words sincere, but just in case a few were still on the fence, I offered a final analogy. "Think of your favorite sports team. You are probably very judgmental and outspoken when they have a bad game or make a terrible trade. Well, that's how it is for me when I think about countries and politics. I am very critical, but not less in love with 'my team.'

"So wrapping up today's Do Now: I love the DR—its people, the culture, and especially their food. In fact, there's nothing I would enjoy more than to be eating their flag right now." A few eyes lit up, while other students looked puzzled. I had a volunteer explain, with lip-smacking animation, that "the flag" is the nickname given to the traditional Dominican dish of meat (typically chicken, but sometimes beef, fish, goat, or pork), rice, and beans served numerous ways, typically with a salad. Her description led to a debate as to whether *concón* (the crunchy rice stuck at the bottom of the pot) is amazing or possibly the greatest thing ever. As that argument started to intensify, I decided to distract them by asking if anybody had ever eaten green chicken. Their looks of disgust disappeared once I explained that "green chicken" is the nickname given to avocado by poor families who have to use it in place of chicken in "the flag" to get their protein.

I finally tried to end the Do Now so we could move on with the lesson. "In conclusion," I said, "the DR is an amazing country but with setbacks that cause most of its people to struggle on a regular basis. Reality is that the average Dominican worker makes less than fifteen dollars a day. And while it's true that their cost of living is significantly lower than ours, most still live in poverty. Personally, I find it more interesting to learn about a country's multiple layers, and I believe people from the island feel the same way. Take, for example, the song 'El Niágara en Bicicleta' by Juan Luis Guerra. He likens the daily struggle to survive in the DR to crossing Niagara Falls on a bicycle."

Most of my experiences in the Dominican Republic have been through social justice tours run by Kevin LaMastra, my colleague and good friend. He's in his forties and has always reminded me of the lead singer of Green Day but with graying temples. Since Kevin performed at the old CBGB punk club in New York City and deejayed at New Jersey's grimy Fast Lane, I think the comparison fits. Late one night, while we were discussing influential films of our youth, he caught me off guard by mentioning a film I had never heard of called *Billy Jack*, about a Navajo Indian and Vietnam War veteran who sticks up for the community's at-risk and underappreciated students. He seemed disappointed when I said the hockey comedy *Slapshot* was my teenage favorite.

Kevin often talks about the "picture that started everything" with regard to his passion for social justice in the classroom. A local newspaper ran an article about Mexican day laborers who had been promised jobs and places to live before they came to the United States. The paper showed a photo of where one of the men slept—inside a cement mixer.

The article led to a split in Kevin's community, because many people seemed appalled when church leaders and police brought the laborers sandwiches and coffee. That divide cost Kevin some valuable sleep.

Kevin and I have taught at the same school for a decade and a half, and we have partnered to run an extracurricular club, Friends Beyond Borders, for most of those years. Watching him expand the focus of the club—from learning about global issues, to organizing charity events, to bringing educators to a foreign country to befriend those living in extreme poverty, to getting our own students over there—has left me in awe.

Kevin has had a lifelong attraction to Caribbean culture. One of the first stories he ever shared with me was how, for his first time abroad in his late teens, he went to Montego Bay, Jamaica, for a reggae fair in 1982 with less than one hundred dollars in his pocket. When he arrived, his first mission was to find accommodations with a local family who could use the money. The money-changer brought Kevin, in his the Clash T-shirt, to a shantytown and introduced him to a family that tailored homemade dresses and had a jerk chicken stand in their front yard. He became a bit nervous when he noticed that their shower was just a PVC spout, but after the husband and wife graciously offered him their own bedroom and what would be his first taste of beer, Red Stripe, he knew he was in good hands.

The one thing in life Kevin is nearly as passionate about as global issues is music. In fact, I would wager that his favorite day of the year is the one during the student tour each summer when he rounds up the group to show off their musical chops at a random karaoke bar with more locals than Americans. Since my voice is weak, I sneak by with colorful limericks roasting the adults on our trip. It has become a tradition of his to take over the place and then lead several songs on a march back to our ride, which quickly turns into a party bus with loud beats, flashing lights, and aisle dancing.

Kevin's interest in the Dominican Republic came about serendipitously while he was reading *La rue cases-nègres* (also called *Black Shack Alley* or *Sugar Cane Alley*) with his French students about ten years ago. Joseph Zobel's semiautobiographical book focuses on Martinique children working in sugarcane fields in the 1930s. About halfway through reading it, Kevin's students asked if there were still kids who worked in similar conditions. He promised he would find out.

After a quick Internet search, Kevin discovered his answer and much more. He reported his findings during his next class, and, of course, this prompted more questions. Being a clever teacher, Kevin harnessed the students' excitement and used their thoughtful questions to create a class project so they could discover the answers on their own. Each time the students learned something new, they discussed their findings as a group, and deeper questions emerged. As this cycle took on a life of its own and the students uncovered more and more, with stories about the DR being the most popular, Kevin started to realize he was on to something big. Their findings about the sugarcane fields led to stories about poverty, which led to stories about immigration, which led to stories about injustice, which led to stories about deep-rooted racism.

But, while the students were learning about the ugliness of discrimination and writing heartfelt comments about struggling people in developing nations, they would use racist remarks toward others as playful put-downs and not see the hypocrisy. "Students expressed a lot of sympathy for people in the poor countries we researched and wanted to fund-raise immediately, but the next day the same kids would put down others by calling them racist names," Kevin said. "For example, we read one story about how Haitian kids are literally eating mud pies these days to stave off nightly hunger pains, and an hour or two later they would be jokingly shouting 'Dirty Haitian!' or 'Dirty Mexican!' in the hallway at their peers." It was then that Kevin realized that sympathy and charity weren't forging the desired connections, so he shifted toward solidarity.

By the end of the school year, he had stumbled across so many controversial and meaningful stories about the Dominican Republic that resonated with the students and paralleled the middle-school curriculum that he knew he had struck classroom gold.

With the summer to mull it over, it became clear to Kevin that the Dominican Republic was the perfect stage to explore his, his students', and other educators' personal and academic curiosities. He realized there was no better place for him, and what would quickly turn out to be more than a hundred students and teachers from across the United States, to observe the world's biggest issues in one spot. "I wanted to offer them a relatability you cannot get from a book, television, or the Internet," he said. Thanks to the DR's close proximity to the United States and the daily flights out of an airport fifteen minutes from our school, it was economically possible for members of our club to get a front-row seat to experience the injustices most only read about.

Kevin spends eleven months of each year planning the itinerary, which mainly involves endlessly calling and emailing contacts in the Dominican Republic and interested travelers in the United States, from coast to coast. From the moment one tour ends until the next begins, it's a labor of love for him, and the results have gained national attention. In 2009, when Friends Beyond Borders was featured in a few magazines, Kevin was flown out to San Diego, Chicago, and Washington, DC, to sit on educational panels and discuss the importance of multicultural education in the classroom.

My main role in Friends Beyond Borders during the school year is to facilitate activities for the club members that encourage them to work cooperatively on problem-solving tasks, build their leadership skills, and find their voices. I do much of the same when we spend time with teenagers in the Dominican Republic. I believe there is immense value in play, both as an icebreaker and as a way to build connections among people who have just met. When individuals who have known each other for a matter of minutes take part in a silly activity that challenges them to compromise their comfort zones and to rely on one another to reach a goal, it becomes so much easier to engage in meaningful dialogue, because they have seen a part of their peers that rarely surfaces for the rest of the world. When we strip away labels and see one another simply as humans navigating our way through life, who experience similar heartbreaks and appreciate a good laugh, we can do so much more.

As a gift to Kevin and FBB, I decided to create a scholarship for one of our students to take part in the trip each year. Most of them get free or reduced lunches at school, and a trip like this one is typically not within their means. However, I have experienced enough in my lifetime to see the value in paying it forward. I am lucky enough to have won that "lottery at birth." I am not affluent by American standards, but I have the luxury of never letting money influence the big decisions I make.

With this scholarship—Kevin usually finds it more worthwhile to break it into two, or sometimes three or four, partial scholarships—I wanted to give my students the chance to take a trip where they would be working alongside those whose job is to collect plastic bottles at a monstrous garbage dump, where they would see how they felt about river-bathing and bucket showers, and where they would experience an actual Vodou ceremony. I wanted to offer them the proverbial trip of a lifetime, organized by the most incredible educator I have ever met. I wanted to give back a little of what I had been given.

Rich Weber and George Santos

Chapter 2
Any Other Monsters on the Island We Should Know About?

A buen oido, pocas palabras.
(To the good ear, few words suffice.)

Kevin is a fearless advocate for the world's most marginalized people. When someone representing the sugar industry threatened legal action if he went through with his afterschool showing of *The Price of Sugar*—a documentary about Haitian workers in the Dominican Republic, narrated by Paul Newman—he didn't blink. The ultimatum definitely rattled our principal, but Kevin assured her the dispute was solely between the plaintiff and the filmmaker.

For someone who delves into global injustices on a regular basis, Kevin is surprisingly soft-spoken. He urges students and educators to get angry and take action when they see something going on that they don't agree with, locally or globally. I think of him as a calm rebel or, better yet, a quiet agitator. There's definitely a fire inside him, but he has the fortitude to keep it in check. When he speaks with the families of students contemplating the summer tour, they all eventually arrive at the same response: "Can I come, too?" More importantly, they see him as a rational thinker, and that is the quality that makes families comfortable taking the final step.

About a month before our flight in the summer of 2010, Kevin held a meeting to discuss the basics of the tour and answer questions. He began by sharing his background as a teacher: he has always loved learning about different cultures, and being able to teach French has been a dream come true. "Learning French is great because people all over the world speak it—like Haiti, Martinique, and Senegal," he said. "But the textbooks never seemed to explain why these countries were full of Francophones. They never once mentioned how France exploited these countries for more wealth and power." Once Kevin made that connection early in his career, he felt a responsibility to give his students the entire story.

Kevin then spoke about his first time in the Dominican Republic, in 2005, the summer after reading *La rue cases-nègres* with his students, traveling the country with large garbage bags of fund-raised goods. On a bus ride, an elderly, weather-beaten man sat next to him with a pillowcase that wouldn't stay still. Soon, he could hear a chicken gurgling as it darted its head this way and that inside the bag. Since the bus wouldn't take Kevin directly to his destination, he had to rely on a guy with a *motoconcho* (motorcycle taxi) to bring him and his oversized bags. Having seen motorcyclists transport things like refrigerators, families of four, and livestock, he knew he wasn't asking too much.

During that first solo endeavor in the Dominican Republic, Kevin realized right away what he wanted his tour to be like. First, he explained to the students' families, Friends Beyond Borders is not a charity group. "For many people, trying to impact the world starts and stops with charity efforts, without any investigation into the root problems," he said. He then spoke about his conscious effort to teach from the bottom up. "It's more important to learn stories about regular people going above and beyond for their communities than reading about an organization giving aid," he said. "Our trip will be unique because we are going to be meeting with people on the front lines combating extreme poverty. We don't want to just experience poverty, but rather hear firsthand stories of resistance and ordinary heroism."

Most of those in attendance at Kevin's Q&A meeting were left speechless, in a good way. "I believe the starting point for people in our country who want to make a difference should be to realize how lucky they are," Kevin continued. "The next step is to understand why so many others are living in desperate circumstances, to really think about how they got to that point. Finally, try to figure out what you and your government can do so nobody has to live without regular access to life's most basic needs. So, while in the DR, we are going to be working with people who struggle every day—with finances, homes, discrimination. But to counterbalance the tough issues, we will also be hearing stories of hope and courage. And, of course, we'll be hitting the beach, snorkeling over coral reefs, and frolicking under the occasional thirty-foot-high waterfall. I guarantee this will not be a depressing tour, but an uplifting one, and by the end of the trip you will feel refreshed and energized. You'll tweet all about it!"

Having given everyone so much to wrap their minds around, Kevin stepped back to discuss the nuts and bolts of preparing for the trip. The students didn't need any shots, for example, and one hundred dollars would be more than enough spending money. For dress recommendations, he broke things down into three categories: beach, local projects, and casual. The beach was easy—shorts, sandals, and shades. For our local projects, such as working at the garbage dump, Kevin recommended that the students bring durable work gloves and wear pants and sneakers that could get dirty. Casual dress should be cool, neat, and comfortable—long pants and a light, collared shirt for the men. He recommended a light shirt underneath so the overshirt wouldn't get sweaty and stick.

In Dominican cities, men go to great lengths to dress properly and maintain a respectable appearance. Women often wear tight clothes; many believe there's no such thing as too tight. Others maintain that there are distinct class lines, and the tighter the clothes, the lower the social class. When it comes to showing too much skin, though, nearly everyone agrees there's a line.

When the baton was passed my way, I went with what I believe is the most important thing to consider before the trip: "I know it's not fun to think about, but because we will be visiting a developing country, I recommend checking with your doctor before the flight about a particular bathroom situation. For me, I prefer a probiotic like Align to keep my system normal. I've been advised to stay away from antidiarrhea pills because they just seal you up and stop the body from doing what it needs. I do bring antidiarrhea pills with me, but only for an emergency airplane situation. Just like my teaching style, I prefer to be proactive to avoid needing to be reactive."

On the day of our flight, my taxi arrived ten minutes early, which was good because driving in New Jersey, which has the highest population density in the country and probably the deepest potholes, can be unpredictable with traffic and never-ending construction. I arrived at the airport on time, tipped my cabbie (who, for some reason, was insisting on dropping me off at the domestic flights terminal), and took a deep breath as I grabbed my suitcase and backpack. As I approached the check-in counter, it was as if my summer vacation had ground to a halt. The abrupt return to work mode caught me off guard. I was suddenly overwhelmed by how much responsibility I had taken on by assuring my students' families that everything would be fine. Even though Kevin runs the trips, I typically get a few students each year who sign up based on their enjoyment of my class and stories.

It was two hours before takeoff. I looked around the congested airport and didn't see anyone familiar. I don't own a cell phone, so I couldn't make any calls.

My fear of overbooking or losing my aisle seat vanished after I slid my passport through the check-in station. I grudgingly paid twenty-five dollars to check my suitcase and smiled at the attendant who handed me my ticket. I took another look around but still didn't see anyone from our group, so I figured it was best to head toward our gate in case any students were already there. When I got to the waiting area, I saw I was not the first to arrive. One of my former students, who had moved on to high school, was there, and we were quickly taken up in a conversation about his life. As Ever, a Salvadoran with a buzz cut and a fierce grip on political issues, reminisced about his time in middle school, he admitted that he wondered why many of his past teachers were so uptight. He looked up to see if he had crossed a line, but I told him I often wondered the same thing. We had a good laugh and decided to go grab some tea, my treat.

As we were walking toward a café, we noticed most of the group approaching us. Right away, the excitement overcame our morning lethargy. I asked Kevin if everything was going smoothly, and his smile made the answer unnecessary. He and his wife were prepared with all the notarized documents we needed to transport minors out of the country—a step I hear many people overlook.

The trip participants were a mix of current and former students from our middle school and ones from Kevin's home area. For my female students and Kevin's daughter, I had made white and yellow beaded flower necklaces, sort of my variation on leis. The girls glanced at them and feigned delight. I told them I had made the jewelry by hand, but my sarcastic nature made them suspicious. Eventually, I convinced them the necklaces were my own creation, but I think they were a bit too girly for today's teenagers. None would be worn during the trip, but I did notice one serving as a bookmark, which in teenage parlance could be taken as a sort of "thank you."

Soon we were boarding the plane, and I walked behind my students to make sure they all got on. They were surprisingly calm as we took our seats. On my two trips to Italy as a chaperone, the students had acted more like they were in the back of a bus than on an airplane. Perhaps I'm starting to become a veteran at these treks.

There is something surreal about being on a plane with your students, and I am referring not to the anticipation of what's to come, but rather to the awkwardness of melding two frames of mind. The best way to explain it is by comparing it to the look a student gives you when she notices you in a supermarket—worlds colliding.

Fifteen minutes after takeoff, people were starting to move around the cabin. I was doing a headcount and met Kevin in the aisle. We compared numbers but didn't match up, so we started over. This time we each did a front-to-back count and arrived at the same number—the wrong one. Our faces both revealed panic at our first, but certainly not last, hurdle of the day. We counted again, this time with the student lists in our hands. We were missing a student—Alexa, who happened to be one of the four I had told Kevin I would monitor. (Kevin had assigned each of the five adults on the trip three or four students to keep an extra set of eyes on.)

I poked my head into first class, but she wasn't there. We waited by the bathrooms at opposite ends of the plane, but she didn't turn up. Kevin dug into his bag and checked Alexa's seat number. Her chair was empty. Nausea set in. That was when Kevin turned to me, and I answered his unspoken question so he wouldn't feel awkward asking it. "I watched all the students I am in charge of get on the plane. I made sure they all walked in front of me." I didn't mention that I hadn't stood by the door to make sure none got off for whatever reason.

We went up and down the rows a third time and still didn't see her. We started asking the others. No leads. I looked at Kevin, who was taking his cell phone out for our last recourse—contacting home. *Is that even possible up here?* To fight the flood of panic, I went up and down the rows one last time, a bit more assertively and, I'm sure, more obnoxiously. That time, I noticed someone curled up in a ball with a hood covering her face. As I stepped closer, my last hope started to flicker. This mystery person was about the right size and wearing what I convinced myself was the same dark hoodie I remembered Alexa having on earlier. A tap on the shoulder could prove embarrassing if I was wrong, but that didn't matter just then. I whispered her name. Slight movement, a good sign. I whispered louder, and the hood slowly came down, along with my blood pressure. I smiled, asked nonchalantly if everything was all right, and grabbed Kevin's arm to prevent him from making an awkward call home. We breathed a dual sigh of relief, noted each other's sweat marks, and without another word went back to our seats.

I proceeded to enjoy the flight meal and movie, and I was happy that at least the landing was smooth. Once the plane was comfortably on the ground, everyone began clapping boisterously. There were even a few whistles and peace signs waving above the chairs. I joined in the excitement.

Stepping off the plane in Santo Domingo, we were immediately assaulted by the tropical humidity. We were at the airport but seemed to be walking around a wooden corridor on the periphery, which was not part of the main structure and therefore not air-conditioned. After only a few minutes, I already felt my shirt sticking to my skin. But before the heat became unbearable, we entered the main building and were welcomed by a merengue band of four older gentlemen wearing bright green and yellow floral shirts that were nearly as loud as their music. Most notable among their instruments was the *güira*, a foot-long sheet metal cylinder from an oilcan, pocked with holes and held by a handle. The oldest of the group played it by rubbing a two-pronged metal brush back and forth. Several students groped in their bags for their cameras.

We moved smoothly through customs, assisted by well-dressed workers, one smile brighter than the next. But on our way to retrieve our baggage, everything went black.

I began to doubt my hydration level and considered shouting, because maybe I was about to lose consciousness and had a split second for someone to catch me before I collapsed. As I opened my mouth and considered which was more important, a last breath of air or a gasp for help, I picked up on some chatter among my students. Their voices were low, and the surrounding noise was loud, specifically one repeated phrase: *"Se fue la luz!"* But as I blocked out the foreign sounds, I could hear the students better: "What happened to the lights?"

Those words quickly assured me that this was an external issue, and the darkness became easier to navigate as my eyes adjusted. Soon I could make out the silhouettes of people in our group, and once I determined our whereabouts, I realized we had only moved about ten feet since the lights went out. Just then, Kevin called out, "Everything is all right. Blackouts are sort of typical here and usually last only a minute or two. Just relax and enjoy your first moment of cultural assimilation. *Se fue la luz!*" (The lights went out!)

A few snickers from the students and adults lightened the mood, and the lights soon flickered back on.

Upon securing our bags and proving the luggage was ours with the stickers put on our boarding passes back in New Jersey, we made our way to our air-conditioned minibus. While I usually like to bring up the back of the line of students, I knew the bus would have ice-cold water waiting for us, so I took the lead to move things along. As I looked back, I saw that most of the students were moving at a leisurely pace; clearly, they were adjusting to the relaxed island mood. I also noticed that a few were sipping from Dixie-style cups. My mouth dry, I felt a pang of jealousy, no matter how small their cups seemed.

As I headed back to prod them along, however, I was stunned by the blue and red label on the cups. *Brugal?* As I peered in, I saw a dark liquid that appeared to be the product for which the manufacturer Brugal is most famous: rum. We hadn't even reached the road, and we adults were already faced with a major hurdle: how to respond to the lax drinking customs here.

With so many other things to keep track of, from passports to medications, we hadn't wanted to overwhelm the students before the flight, so we had decided that topics such as alcohol and curfew could wait until our orientation at the hotel. We had obviously underestimated the number of potential pitfalls, and that would quickly become a theme for our week on the island.

"Look on the bright side," I told the other adults, whom I had only known for a few hours. "I guess we won't have to worry about doing any icebreakers or get-to-know-you activities today, since alcohol can tear down the walls we build around us much quicker than anything we may have had in mind." Strangely, that comment earned me no smiles.

As we exchanged looks of concern, an invisible game of hot potato took place. Nobody seemed eager to spell out alcoholic parameters just yet. Luckily, before any real tensions arose, we noticed a tall, bald German-American man holding a clipboard sign reading "Friends Beyond Borders." Having previously worked with Rich—a thirty-six-year-old father of one with a second on the way, well known on the island for his zany smile, hearty laugh, and backward sunglasses look—I finally felt I could let my guard down and start breathing normally again.

In addition to arranging the accommodations and transportation as the ground operator for Kevin's social justice tours, Rich, who was trained as a wilderness first responder at Cornell University and previously served as the administrative director of the Council on International Education, is now the CEO of Tours Trips Treks & Travel, organizing a multitude of adventure excursions on the island for clients from rock bands to magazine writers. While he had assigned us one of his most dependable guides, we learned from previous teacher tours that he also tweaked his own schedule so he could be with us for the first couple of days, because he admires our unique reason for being in the Dominican Republic.

When we reached the bus, Rich introduced us to the driver and Yunior, whom the students connected with right away due to his youthful exuberance. Yunior, a thirty-six-year-old who looks twenty-six, is a *campesino* (one who lives in a rural setting) who could easily afford a more upscale lifestyle but chooses to embrace his roots. He is on the short and skinny side and impressed all of us with his suaveness and his way around the English language. As Yunior and the driver handled our luggage, Rich introduced himself to each person and handed out bottles of water. As we settled into our seats, I peered out the window and saw several vans with the names of resorts stenciled on the side picking up tourists. The window shades on our bus were wide open, while theirs were closed. I found this very symbolic in that we wanted our students to look behind the curtains and question their surroundings—to realize there is a design in place for visitors not to see certain things while on the island.

Boarding the bus, I thought back to my first time in the Dominican Republic in 2007. As I checked out the street action—women getting their hair done; men barbecuing chicken using metal oil barrels cut in half and painted in their flag's red, white, and blue; and children chasing chickens—I became nervous that I would find myself in compromised situations because I didn't speak Spanish fluently. During this minianxiety attack, I was looking out the window at the colorful stores. The first few establishments I noticed were a *floristería*, a *dentistería*, and a *mecánica*. The signs brought a wave of relief—this might be easy after all. The next store, though, left me confounded: *ferretería*. Could there possibly be a store that specialized in ferrets? Well, that might be fun to check out, *unless* Dominicans hold the ferret in the same regard as Peruvians hold the guinea pig, as one of the priciest meals on the menu. I was too embarrassed to ask for clarification, but we soon passed another *ferretería*—there is no shortage of them—and I realized they were more or less small versions of Home Depot.

Back in the present, the bus doors slammed shut, the driver pulled away, and we were off. Leaving behind the airport and the countless cabbies stealing some shade while flirting with any *chica* (cute young lady) who walked by, we were welcomed by cloudless skies, palm trees, and gentle guitar plucks from a bachata[3] tune over the radio. Kevin grabbed the microphone, let a few well-known rap lyrics fly, and went into his spiel.

"Well, first off, I would like to officially welcome you to the Dominican Republic—the country of 'God, mom, and baseball.' A country where children learn to dance before they walk." The students clapped, and several cheered. "Thank you," Kevin said, with a smile that seemed unhampered by the heat. He reintroduced Rich, Yunior, and the driver. "I just want to go over a few things before we arrive at our accommodations in Santo Domingo's Colonial Zone, which should be in about twenty-five minutes. Number one, if you haven't yet received something to drink or would like another bottle of water, please ask. We need you to be hydrated at all times. The heat here can be tricky in that you might feel cool, but your body knows the actual temperature. Let's put it this way: When you actually start feeling thirsty, it's too late, and you are already on the road to dehydration. With that, please don't use any tap water, not even for brushing your teeth. Plumbing here has its issues, and lots of bacteria get into the water. It is safe to shower with, as long as you aren't the type who likes to open your mouth and let the water flow in."

"Since we are on the topic of plumbing, you should also know that in the DR they don't flush toilet paper." This comment caught the attention of the students who were peering out the window, pointing at a truck carrying a dozen restless pigs packed tightly together. "After toilet paper is used, it is disposed of in the trash cans." That prompted a moment of silence and wide-eyed, open-mouthed glances at neighbors. Many students then let out a noise that seemed one part laugh and two parts "Egad!"

"My final tip until orientation is to make sure that those with fair skin, like myself, reapply sunscreen throughout the day," Kevin said. "The sun burns quickly, and we don't want to miss any exciting moments due to a rough burn." One student said he had brought surfer shirts designed to block the sun. I did research when we returned to the States and learned that several popular clothing brands now offer special UPF casual shirts, too. I added these to my list of things to pack next

---

[3] Bachata is referred to as *musica del amargue* (bitter music). For instance, in Héctor Acosta's song "Tu Veneno" ("Your Poison"), he says that "you give love and in return you get the thorns," "I'm going to burn our last photo," and "I'm going to force you out of my heart, until none of your poison remains in my blood."

time, because my shoulders have gotten burned badly in the Dominican Republic despite wearing a light shirt.

As we arrived at the hotel, Kevin gave out room pairings. We got the students their keycards, gave them our room numbers and hotel business cards in case they got lost while wandering nearby, and told them that we would meet in the lobby in one hour for a brief orientation.

The adults were last to get their keys from the receptionist, and when I heard my name called I was suddenly short of breath again. The voice belonged to the most beautiful woman I have ever encountered, bar none. I once read that hundreds of years ago, some people in the Amazon jungle had such an abundance of gold that they would crush it into a powder and cover their bodies with the dust. I was convinced that this radiant, toned beauty must be one of their descendants.

"*Hola, mi amor*," she said. Fortunately, or perhaps unfortunately, I knew what that meant: "Hello, my love." While I have been told numerous times that this is a common greeting for Dominican women, it left me weak-kneed. I mumbled something because I didn't want to seem strange, but as soon as I did, I had no idea what I had just said. I couldn't even tell if I had answered in English or Spanish. Perhaps it was French. She placed a keycard in my hand, and I stared from her fingers up to her big, dark eyes. I gulped. I managed to utter a *gracias*, and she responded with a *de nada*. With one last look, I peered at her blouse and caught her name. Yudelkis. Most likely a hybrid of Yudith and Belkis to pay homage to loved ones.

Then I found myself outside my fourth-floor room, though I couldn't remember taking an elevator. (I always opt for higher floors in the DR because both of the tarantula scares we had on previous trips took place in ground-floor rooms.) When I tried to use my keycard, it didn't work. I tried again; nothing. Luckily, Kevin was next door and noticed my frustration. He said that oftentimes the keycards needed to be reset by the receptionist. I could only look at him with pitiful eyes. He might have understood my desperation, or maybe he thought I didn't want to leave my bags. Either way, he said he would run down for me. I was certainly in no condition to request another key from *mi amor*.

Kevin returned, and I pushed the card in with my eyes closed. The lock clicked. I pulled my luggage into the room, and Kevin asked if I

The Dominican Experiment

wanted to run to an ATM.[4] He said the other adults were hanging out in the lobby, and it would probably be our only free time until tomorrow to get money and a couple of gallons of bottled water to keep in our fridges.

Leaving the hotel and its precious air-conditioning, we took to the bustling streets of Santo Domingo. The colossal casinos along the shore were convenient landmarks that helped me keep my bearings. We briefly strolled the sweltering capital and took in reggaeton music blasting from unseen radios. As I started bobbing to the music, I heard a few "Pssst, pssst!" *piropos* (catcalls) directed at us from two waving young ladies. I had learned from previous trips that they were probably not sex workers, just your average, forward females looking for an American friend. I used a tip I had learned from Kevin and tried not to communicate any interest by making eye contact or other gestures; I just continued moving to the music. Luckily, I had mastered his number one rule of safety—avoid engagement—and we were left alone.

As we were walking, a fellow American wearing an iPod passed us on the street, and Kevin shook his head in disbelief. "How can you not fall in love with the city sounds?" he asked. "The blasting tunes, purposely loud motorcycles, and trucks with speakers taped to roofs chanting monotone rock-bottom prices for the fruit, vegetables, or mattresses rising high above their truck beds—this is what makes it feel real for me." Digging into a bag of *chicharrón de cerdo* (fried pork rinds) decorated with a cartoon pig, he then gave me an impromptu lesson on distinguishing bachata from merengue music[5]: guitar strumming is the centerpiece of bachata, while merengue has a beat for small steps tracing back to shackled slaves' limited movement.

As we neared a small grocery store with an ATM out front, I grabbed Kevin's arm. A rugged, middle-aged man was leaning alongside the ATM with a shotgun dangling by his side. While I had seen this before, there is just no getting used to pulling out your bank card, plugging in your password, and withdrawing thousands of pesos while

---

[4] I recommend not using an ATM on weekends because it might run out of money but still deduct the amount requested from your account. I've also heard rumors that they sometimes give counterfeit money.

[5] During his dictatorship, Rafael Trujillo banned bachata (due to its lower class origins) and made merengue the country's official music.

a man with a firearm glares over your shoulder. Dominicans refer to these men as *guachimanes* or *guachis* (watchmen) and say they are there to protect the machines. I would much prefer if they said they were there to protect the customers.

Having produced yet another adrenaline cocktail, we returned to the hotel a few minutes before orientation. I am a big fan of Rich's no-holds-barred approach to introducing life on the island to teachers, and I wondered how similar his approach would be with our students.

We gathered in the lounge area, overflowing with framed portraits of chickens—perhaps they were famous *pollos*—which a handful of mosquitoes had figured out was a human rest stop.[6]

Later in the week, we would pass through a highway toll and receive a colorful handout on the dangers of mosquitoes. The key message of the flier was not to leave tires lying around, because water collects on the inside and creates a perfect breeding ground for mosquitoes, which can carry malaria, West Nile virus, or dengue fever. I've never heard of anyone contracting malaria in the Dominican Republic, but I have heard some rough stories about long stays in the hospital because of dengue fever.

Yunior, with his short, curly hair and permanently wet look, started orientation with a simple greeting in Spanish over Kevin's soft bachata music in the background. He then moved on to a geography warm-up, asking two students to hold the ends of a poster map for all to see and quizzing the group on some general facts.

"So we are currently in Santo Domingo, the nation's capital. Can someone tell me where that is on the map?" A student got up and pointed

---

[6] I often tease Kevin that, over our four weeks on the island—eight days for the student tour, twelve days to recuperate and plan, eight days for the teacher tour—his legs can serve as a time line of our travels. Near the ocean, you don't get many mosquitoes because they need stagnant water to lay their eggs, but more days spent inland, and he will have various trails of blood intersecting on his legs. The more winding the trails, the longer and deeper he was inland. From aloe vera (which, when a leaf falls off, also serves as a detector of bad energy in homes) to bananas to pharmacy pills, Dominicans are not short on ways to remedy the bites and prevent infection.

to the southern coast. "And what body of water does the southern coast border?" Another student correctly answered the Caribbean Sea.

"Later in the week, we will be at the northern part of the country in Puerto Plata," Yunior said. "Can someone tell me what body of water Puerto Plata borders?" A few students gave the correct answer, the Atlantic Ocean. "Each year, from January to March, thousands of humpback whales migrate from the waters near Canada, Greenland, and Iceland to the Samaná Peninsula in the northeast of the DR for an annual pilgrimage to their ancestral breeding grounds," he continued, and the parents nodded in approval as he revealed a series of gems you wouldn't find in the typical travel book—like the fact that Samaná was a popular destination in the early 1800s for freed slaves from the United States.

"My last note is about Dominican communication," he said. "We tend to be very direct with our words if we are trying to get your attention and don't know your name. So if someone on the street calls you *flaca* (skinny), *morena* (brown-skinned), *pequeña* (short), or *rubia* (blonde), try not to take offense. As for being called *gorda* (fat), many Dominicans take it as a compliment. 'That's right; I can afford to feed my family' is a comment they may retaliate with.

"We Dominicans also like to eat the *s* at the beginning and end of our words. Words like *gracias* become *gracia*; *buenos días* (good day) becomes *buen día*; and *estoy bien* (I am well) becomes *toy bien*.

"As for nonverbal communication, Dominicans make an art of it. The mouth puckered to one side means to check this person out. Puckered forward is like pointing straight. Wrinkling of the nose indicates that they didn't hear or understand you. Grabbing of the ear means you think somebody is crazy. And a cupping of the elbow is declaring a person to be cheap. These are done slightly and quickly, so they may go unnoticed."

The students found those last tips fascinating, so Yunior went a step further. "When playing dominos, one of our national pastimes, you might catch a lot of signals thrown at their partners. If they have a blank piece, they will touch their teeth to symbolize all white. To represent a two, a player will cross his two arms. A six will likely have a player rubbing his curly hair." The students applauded when Yunior concluded and comically took a bow.

Rich has a unique personal history with the Dominican Republic that began with a study abroad program. He has lived on the island for fifteen years, with all his past jobs touching on three areas in one way or another: adventure, community service, and education. When it was his turn to address the group, he gave what he called a "geopolitical history of the island." He cleared his throat and, in his most professorial voice and with perfect posture, told the students that the island was formed not by volcanoes, but tectonically, meaning that plates crashed together and thrust upward. Rich then added, with a hint of seriousness, staring at us adults, that the country still has active fault lines.

"Hispaniola used to be two separate islands until they merged, leaving a trail of scattered lakes as evidence of the union," he said. "The DR makes up the eastern two-thirds of the island and is about the size of Vermont and New Hampshire combined. It shares the island with Haiti and has the most clearly defined border of any two neighboring countries when flying overhead." He informed us that the island was originally called Quisqueya, an indigenous word said to mean "mother of all lands." He gestured to the map and pointed at three mountain ranges: the Central, Oriental, and Septentrional. "No, the DR is not just made up of beaches like many people seem to think and dress," he said, glancing my way—revealing an obvious pet peeve, and possibly a hint that I needed to stop looking like a tourist lost in the city. "There are more than twenty different climate zones here, which include desert landscapes, tropical valleys, and pine forests.

"The DR is home to the highest and lowest elevations of the Caribbean islands: the mountain Pico Duarte in the Cordillera Central, and the giant saltwater lake Lago Enriquillo.[7] Pico Duarte is named after Juan Pablo Duarte, one of the three founding fathers who helped the DR gain independence from Haiti in 1844.[8] Pico Duarte was once called Pico Trujillo, after the infamous dictator. Enriquillo is also a popular seltzer water on the island, but more importantly, he was a famous Taíno Indian who led a slave revolt against the Spaniards in the 1500s."

---

[7] Lago Enriquillo, the largest lake in the Caribbean, has nearly doubled in size over the past decade.

[8] In Dominican schools, their independence is highlighted as their breaking away from Haiti, not Spain.

Kevin's eyes lit up when the Taíno were mentioned. "If I may jump in," he said, "I think one of your goals during this week should be to watch for the following cultural influences on the island: African, Spanish, and Taíno. You'll see it all around you, especially when we get to the Centro León museum in Santiago."

After Kevin's interjection, Rich switched gears and addressed the nature of the tour. "All excursions were planned with personal safety, cultural sensitivity, and our environmental impact in mind," he assured the group. "What you are taking part in is an experiential learning trip. You are in a position of privilege and have the luxury to examine other cultures, and even change them. I think of you as ambassadors from the United States, here to observe, connect with the people, and bring back stories to your friends and families." As he spoke, an empowered look grew on the students' faces. Rich then added an endorsement for Kevin, saying the students were lucky to have him as a tour leader because he had developed a lot of *confianza* ("street cred") over the years.

Rich concluded with a quick activity that looked at first like an impromptu game of musical chairs but would become a demonstration on personal space. He invited four students to sit in four chairs at the front of the room. They started to fidget immediately, because each chair was touching the next and there was little wiggle room. After they had found comfortable positions, Rich invited another four to join them, without adding any more chairs. The seated students stared at the ones standing with body language that unmistakably called for them to get their own chairs. But with a bit of prodding—and a cultural explanation that in the DR, eight can easily fit in a row meant for four, and Dominicans employ a "just look forward" technique to respect people seated close by—the students had fun making room for the others to squeeze in.

When I first tried to recruit students for the trip, many thought it was going to be a partner exchange. We would have loved to do a home-stay swap trip like I did with Italian families years ago, but Rich told us up front that it would be nearly impossible to pull that off, what with the countless hurdles Dominicans face when they apply for visas. We did use that as a teachable moment, asking the students why it was so much easier for us to get up and go to another country than it was for Dominicans. Many of the students echoed Rich's recently mentioned idea of "privilege," and Kevin nodded in approval.

Rich then spoke briefly about the rules of the road. "In the Dominican Republic, size matters. Chickens and small children are on the bottom rung and have to get out of the way of all others," he said, to the students' amusement. He concluded by listing seven things he expected each of us to have during our travels: water bottle, sunblock, bug repellant, rain gear, personal snacks, flashlight, and toilet paper. The students rolled their eyes at the mention of yet another bathroom hurdle.

Next up was Kevin's fifteen-minute crash course on the Dominican Republic. He began with a twist: "Can anybody tell me who Tony Montana was?" The students wrinkled their brows and started to look around at one another. "He was the main character in the movie *Scarface*," Kevin said. "But more importantly, he's the nickname many corner-side drug dealers use when trying to sell marijuana or a host of other illegal substances and services from their mopeds." A chorus of ahs went out. "Of course, I don't expect anybody to be partaking in illegal activities on this trip. But you should know that the catch is that when these Tonys sell their target some drugs, minutes later they call their cousins, who happen to be on the local police force, and then the mark is picked up and shaken down for possession. Would someone like to clarify that last part for me?"

"Yeah. It means they set you up, and the cop is going to take whatever money you have in your wallet as a bribe to keep you from being booked," a student offered.

"Exactly!" I said. "Plus, he'll likely stop by an ATM so he can make the whole affair really worth his time and energy."

Years ago, a documentary called *Scared Straight* was filmed at Rahway State Prison (near where I grew up in New Jersey), that showed the happenings of prison life. For many teens, it was a reality check that prison is not the least bit alluring, as Hollywood sometimes portrays it. There's a new version called *Beyond Scared Straight* that often focuses on female prisons, and many of my students say it's their favorite television show. Kevin took a much milder approach than these films, but when in a foreign country with many ways to go astray, it is better to give too many warnings than too few.

"Next, I want to talk to you about the devil that lives here on the island," Kevin said. Immediately, the students' eyes darted out. *What exactly did we sign up for?* "The devil lives in your hotel room." A few students gasped. "*El diablo* also goes by the names refrigerator and minibar." At this point the students were catching on that, after the long flight, Kevin was just throwing in a little drama mixed with humor to ensure they remembered his key points. "The prices of the items are marked up 300 percent or more and are often stale, so avoiding them would be wise." He then rambled on about the six-dollar Milky Way he had last time that was memorable for the wrong reason.

A student called out, "Any other monsters on the island we should know about?"

"Actually, yes," Kevin said. "The devil has a cousin who also lives at the hotel. His name is *el teléfono*, and his rates are even more frightening."

After his *Scared Straight in the DR* opening, Kevin took a much lighter tone. He discussed the benefits of carrying small change such as twenty and fifty pesos, so you're not relying on merchants for correct change.[9] Many vendors will pretend not to have exact change in hopes that Americans will tell them to keep the money owed. Others might suddenly speak much less English and rely on buyers' impatience with the linguistic confusion to make them give up and go away. Kevin threw in a second reminder to stay hydrated: "On average, the body can sweat two liters of water in an hour, but only absorb one." Lastly, he told the students that the occasional loose stool was common, as I had graphically described at the Q&A meeting before the trip, but to inform an adult if it got past that stage. On that note, he reminded them sardonically about his number one rule on the trip: don't get sick. He noted that the most common way visitors get sick on the island is water consumption, and the second is sun exposure.

Noticing the students' weariness and realizing he had covered the most important bases, Kevin stopped. "Okay, I think that is enough information for one night. Who is ready to eat?" After the exhausting flight and unsettling introduction, some students looked like they'd rather call home for a comforting voice than eat dinner where the next monster might be lurking.

As the students started to grab their gear, Kevin asked if I had any quick words. I decided to plant a few seeds before they took to the streets.

---

[9] Another benefit of carrying small bills is to avoid the looks of disgust from vendors when you hand them a 1,000-peso bill for something that cost one hundred pesos—many regard the act as a personal offense.

"Before we go to eat, I just want to say three really quick things. First off, when I brought students to Italy, they received a similar orientation speech to the one you just heard." I figured that misery loves company and that letting them know this sort of speech was a universal talk might make it less intimidating. "Secondly, judge slowly. You are going to experience quite a bit of culture shock this week, and I recommend trying not to be judgmental and instead ask questions. Lastly, this week will be the ultimate test of your comfort zones.[10] We'll discuss that more in depth later in the week. Now, we eat! *Buen provecho!*"

We were off to eat our first dinner at a nearby restaurant, and spirits were high. A few students had even joyfully locked arms, and their chain was growing by the minute. Soon the twenty-five of us were seated around a few tables pushed together so we could dine as a group. The waitress was making her rounds, taking our drink orders and marking which of the three meal options each of us would prefer.[11]

Only minutes after we took our seats, street vendors were on the scene, tempting our students with their wares. I was confident the teens would make us proud, mostly because they hadn't had a chance to exchange their currency yet. When the first man brought by flowers, the students were stoic and didn't engage, following our advice that ignoring a vendor isn't rude and saves him time. Next came the artworks. The students seemed tempted but glanced our way and then down. Last came a mystery box, and the students caved within seconds. When I got up to see what this clever merchant had in his possession that had broken down our best defenses and had our students oohing and awing, I had to laugh. Once again, our attempt to be a few steps ahead of the game had been dismantled—by a box of month-old puppies. (Having seen boxes of chicks for sale at ten pesos [twenty-five cents] each, I shouldn't have been caught off guard.) "There'll be time for souvenirs later in the week" was the best I could come up with at the moment. I considered adding that it was better to wait until the end of the trip for

---

[10] The biggest test of my comfort zone on the trip was trying to use a bathroom (which was connected to the family's busy kitchen) with a bed sheet serving as a door.

[11] It was brilliant thinking on Kevin's part to narrow the students' dining choices to three—a meat, fish, or vegetable dish—to prevent confusion and save time. He also included all meals in the price of the tour so we could make smooth transitions without money issues tying us up.

shopping because things might break or get lost in the hustle and bustle, but a dog licking a student's face was a worthy adversary.

After bringing drinks around for everybody, a young Dominican waitress headed to my part of the table. I was taken by how much she resembled Yudelkis, my friendly hotel receptionist. Strangely, a lot of the *chicas* during the week would. She came over to take my order and asked how I was, so I tried to model immersion for the students by speaking Spanish and said the first thing that came to my mind: *"Estoy caliente."* Her body language gave me immediate feedback, but not the kind I had expected, which told me she probably didn't understand my broken comment. Instead, she briefly caressed my shoulder and offered a small gesture with her lips. Being that Dominicans are so expressive with their lips, I wondered if her gesture had a deeper meaning. Before I had time to ask Yunior what she was trying to tell me, I noticed that Kevin had a big grin on his face. He asked what I had said to her, or better yet, what I thought I had said to her.

"I just commented on the weather. She asked how I was, so I told her I was hot," I said with fading confidence. Kevin's grin grew into a laugh.

"Yeah, you told her you were hot, all right. Hot for her!" A few students overheard Kevin's interpretation and had a good chuckle at my expense, which would become yet another theme.

Embarrassment started to set in, but I tried to tell myself it was an innocent mistake. I looked over, intending to apologize to the waitress, but she immediately repeated the small, kiss-like gesture. It seemed more friendly than seductive, but that offered me no real comfort. Nobody else seemed to notice it, so I decided to pull my chair in closer to the table and ask the students what they thought so far about Santo Domingo.

A batey man who asked to have his picture taken

Chapter 3
HELL ON EARTH

No es lo mismo llamar al diablo, que verlo llegar.
(It is not the same to call the devil over, than to see him coming.)

My friends know it simply as my favorite place on the planet. A teacher whom I roomed with on a previous social justice tour clung to the expression "hell on earth" each time we visited one. But I couldn't disagree more. I challenged him to find one other spot on earth that offers so much authenticity. Of all the photographs I share with my students, it's the ones of this place they are most moved by—the wiry father stacking car tires to build a fire for dinner, children lugging gallons of potable water in worn plastic bottles, homes without numbers, and streets without signs. I don't think it's a contradiction to find so much beauty in such a downtrodden place.

My first time rolling up to a batey (a sugar workers' town), hidden within endless fields of neglected sugarcane, I came face to face with the shantytown homes of Haitian migrant workers and their descendants. You drive up expecting these people to be overcome by their circumstances, but the life in their eyes never fades. A pearly smile from a woman taking a bucket shower on her front porch so she can keep an eye on her children doing the naked dance; the centennial grandfather who pulls out plastic chairs so you can chat comfortably on a makeshift porch while waiting out a sudden, deafening storm; the girls pulling discarded oil quarts cleverly converted into toy cars with open roofs to transport random playthings, and the boys using sticks with handles from bleach containers to push bicycle wheels around—I see it as life without the phoniness, and it couldn't be more beautiful.

The homes many batey squatters live in were designed in the 1940s and 1950s, during Rafael Trujillo's reign, and are eerily reminiscent of slave ship accommodations—the number of people per room determined by how many adults can lie side by side. Nowadays, between four and twelve people live in each home, approximately the size of the average US classroom.

The most frequent question I get back home when talking about the tour is, "Do you go there to build homes or schools?" To which I respond, "No. We go there to build relationships." (It would be the batey residents with whom our students would make the strongest connections during the trip.) Besides, even if we wanted to build homes or schools for them, many people living in bateys are hesitant to accept such offers by humanitarian groups because there are often strings attached to the "free" structures—and even when there aren't, the government owns the land, so there is still risk involved.

From 1950 to 1960, there were three labor agreements between the Dominican Republic and Haiti to bring workers across the border. The Haitian workers who signed up were led to believe they were starting a new life, but when they arrived in the DR, they quickly noticed the armed guards. Just before the turn of the twenty-first century—when the sugar industry on the island was brought to its knees by a global "race to the bottom" for lower wages, and the jobs moved mainly to Brazil—the cane fields closed, prompting mass deportations of Haitians. Adding insult to injury, the workers were not given their last payments, and the factories were left in place, casting jagged shadows as constant reminders of their oppression. In the haphazard removal of Haitians, Dr. Ana Celia Carrero, the program director of the Batey

Relief Alliance,[12] who had silky raven hair and spoke with audacity, told us there was a common theme of "families being displaced, loved ones being separated, and women being raped."

At the peak of the sugar industry, there were around five hundred bateys in the Dominican Republic. Only about half are still occupied. Those workers who haven't been rounded up live a wayward life. The Batey Relief Alliance (BRA)—which has a cartoon condom at its entrance reminding those who pass through, *"Usame, yo te protejo"* ("Use me, I protect you")—is nestled next door to one of the country's lively bateys, and it helps provide residents of that and many other bateys with safe drinking water and plumbing. At its clinic, the organization treats two hundred to three hundred patients each day, including many after its scheduled closing time. During our visit, its records showed that thirty-nine thousand people had received treatment in the past six months. BRA, which is the first and only modern medical facility in a batey, is also responsible for providing sixty-five thousand children with antiparasite medication and supplemental vitamins twice a year. While several bateys are close by, people on the outskirts of the island travel for hours by bus, motorcycle, and horse, or for days on foot, to see a doctor.

Recently, BRA embarked on a project in Monte Plata, in the central part of the country, where it purchased thirty acres of land to grow crops such as pineapple, yucca, and potatoes, with the dual purpose of employing batey residents and educating them about nutrition.

BRA also holds regular workshops on contraceptives and pregnancy. Since church and state are closely tied in the Dominican Republic, the group isn't allowed to distribute condoms during church-sponsored workshops. At its clinic, run by doctors (fifteen to twenty are employed during the average month) and interns from the Dominican Republic, Canada, and the United States, it is less restricted. Twenty percent of patients are expected to pay a nominal fee for treatment, while 80 percent have a "card of solidarity," which goes to batey children, pregnant women, and HIV/AIDS patients after a census and means the government will cover their fees.

Wherever you have ramshackle homes, you have unreliable resources. Those homes with electricity have it because people spliced one of the dozens of dangerously tangled power lines, which too often

---

[12] BRA is also active in Haiti and Peru.

lead to electrocutions. I've even seen the web of sloppy wiring cause electrical fires. I remember this event clearly because I physically had to stop my students from running over for a closer look.

Added to the electrical problems are those of simple safety. "They are looking for peace but cannot find it because there's no true security where they live," Dr. Carrero said. I tried to imagine the toll it must take on an individual to live in complete insecurity every day. "The police avoid bateys. They don't leave the batey after dark because they have to protect their stuff, and it's dangerous even to go out and use the bathroom." The bathrooms are typically narrow metal shacks containing just a wooden bench with a hole over a pit. There is no light bulb, and you quickly realize that the buzzing sound above is from wasp nests along the flimsy roof.

Most Haitians born in the Dominican Republic are not given birth certificates because they are labeled transients.[13] Even those who are able to obtain a birth certificate because of connections or high status live in constant fear because of past rulings that retroactively made birth certificates invalid if an individual's parents weren't considered legitimate Dominican citizens.[14] According to BRA, 20 percent of the ten million people living in the Dominican Republic are undocumented, trapped in a vicious cycle of poverty.[15]

The hurdles for Haitians living in the Dominican Republic begin at birth and grow exponentially. Because children born on bateys do not receive birth certificates, they cannot obtain identification. Living without documentation severely limits people's ability to meet their basic needs. Without an ID, there is very limited access to education, health care, or judicial review. Since most people living in bateys are stateless, when one leaves the batey for a day, there is always the fear

---

[13] Unlike the US, which automatically grants citizenship to anyone born within its borders, the DR Constitution states that if a newborn's parents are "illegal residents" or "in transit," that child is not considered a citizen of the country.

[14] The people whose birth certificates were invalidated were told to go to Haiti to get new ones, but they couldn't because those documents must be obtained during the first two years of a child's life—plus, many of them had never been to Haiti.

[15] Refugees International also estimates that 20 percent of the people living in the DR are undocumented.

that he might never come back. "Even if you graduated college and own a home, if you are Haitian, you are still at risk." When we asked if things were improving, Dr. Carrero told us, "Every day, more doors get closed to Haitians."

While Dr. Carrero was speaking metaphorically, her words reminded me of the night we went clubbing in Santo Domingo with a Peace Corps worker. As we neared the hot spots, our guide said our options were much more limited than they appeared because the white Peace Corps worker's black boyfriend was "too dark" to be allowed into several clubs. That was the summer of 2008. The place we settled on, and are drawn back to each year, is a loud spot with older, well-dressed men who quickly scoop up our youngest as dance partners before they could sit in one of the plastic chairs in a portion of the street sectioned off by four beat-up orange cones. Our improvised VIP spot is in front of an oddly vandalized door with countless fours inscribed in bizarre shapes and styles befitting a Stephen King novel—an eerie way to remind passersby of the movement for the country to fulfill its promise to spend 4 percent of its gross domestic product on education.

When it comes to views on race, women, and sexuality, too many people in the Dominican Republic are stuck in the 1950s. On one teacher tour, a lesbian couple requested a king bed, the same as two heterosexual couples. When Kevin brought the heterosexual couples to the front desk, they were given keycards, smiles, and nods. When he motioned the lesbian couple forward, they were given ignorance. Kevin showed the hotel worker the roster that listed who had double beds and who had single beds, but the worker played dumb—or perhaps he wasn't playing. The two women were told to wait while the hotel figured out "the problem."

According to Dr. Carrero, the first bateys were built in 1901 and designed to be "very closed communities, like prisons." They were "created very far apart, strategically by the owners, so as not to have access or communication with others if a revolution was brewing."

Bateys were constructed with one objective in mind: the cheap processing of sugarcane. Sugarcane is not indigenous to the island; Christopher Columbus, the first governor of Hispaniola, brought it over as a potential cash crop on his second trip to the Caribbean in

1493, realizing Taíno gold would eventually run out.[16] Before sugarcane became dominant, hunger and malnutrition were unheard of in the Dominican Republic because subsistence farming was widespread and diversified. To this day, Dominicans are very proud of their land. "Our land is so fertile that if you spit on the ground, in a few days you will have a spit tree," George Santos, tour guide extraordinaire and coauthor of this book, often jokes.

When Haitians were first brought over to the sugarcane fields, only the men were hired. The corporations expected that the women would follow their husbands, and they did—but since the companies hadn't invited the women, they felt no responsibility toward them, leaving them and their children with no access to health care. As expected, the women soon took up cooking and cleaning to support their families while their husbands toiled with machetes all day under the hot sun, making it even more cost effective for the sugar companies to operate.[17]

Another trademark of a batey is the ubiquitous presence of children who love to entertain and be entertained, and seem relatively unhampered by their plight. Sixty percent of those living in bateys are children, and the motto of a batey could easily be, "It takes a village to raise a child." When humanitarian groups build schools, about 70 percent of the children attend. They are the most vulnerable of all the batey residents, but they also have the most potential. As for adolescents, Dr. Carrero told us that few older teens lived in bateys. Instead, she said, "they take off for cities to work at resorts."

Most people in bateys do not see themselves as needing help. Quite the opposite, they go above and beyond to make sure we feel welcomed. On one occasion, two gentlemen fetched a mattress from one of their homes for a student of ours who was sick. In the first chapter, I gave the first three words that come to my mind when I think of the Dominican Republic from my perspective as a teacher, when I view the country as

---

[16] Sugar from the island would go on to become so valuable that, for a while, it was measured by the gram.

[17] Analogous to the sugar industry on the island is the garment industry, which has also seen many factories close because work can be done more cheaply in places such as China—where workers are paid about forty cents an hour, work twelve hour shifts (seven days a week), and where there are suicide nets around the factories' upper floors.

a forest. But as a human, looking within that forest and studying the trees, three other words surface when I think about Dominicans as people: affectionate, family-oriented, and generous. (Seemingly built into the DNA of Dominicans is the inability to say no to a favor.)

Another major advocate for batey residents is MUDHA (Movimiento de Mujeres Dominico Haitiana, or the Haitian-Dominican Women's Movement). One of its main objectives is to help children get birth certificates and provide them with school uniforms, supplies, and breakfast programs. MUDHA workers say the top two problems batey residents face are the lack of safe drinking water and identification. They also say that there is "only one way in and one way out of a batey."

MUDHA was founded in 1983, during a national feminist movement, and was led by Sonia Pierre, the "Cesar Chavez of the Haitian migrant workers," until her untimely death in 2011. Sonia grew up on the Lechería batey in Villa Altagracia and learned early on about the exploitation of her people when she was jailed at the age of thirteen for acting as a translator during a successful five-day sugarcane workers' strike over living conditions, equipment, and back pay. I had the good fortune to meet Sonia, who was tall with strong features and a motherly smile. Her daughter Manuela once shared her mother's story with us: "The sugarcane workers laid down in the fields and stopped working for the day." When the owner and police showed up, out from the fields marched a little girl, who stated the strikers' demands and was arrested. When Manuela asked her mother what was going through her mind back then, Sonia answered, "A strike is the way authorities will listen to people."

Sonia received her elementary schooling from volunteers under the shade of a batey tree. "She never thought she'd be a defender of human rights, because she always thought she'd be a fashion model," Manuela said. That was because fashion magazines were among the only reading materials available on her batey. Nonetheless, after that first taste of activism, Sonia went on to choose Cuba as the ideal place to study social movements and develop her vision.

"She didn't care what price she had to pay to win this struggle," said Leticia, Sonia's other daughter. Leticia informed us about the time Manuela was told she hadn't gotten the role of Minerva Mirabal in a school production because of her color, to which her mother responded, "That's why I come home late." And on those rare days when Sonia was home early, Leticia recalled with a smile, her four children did their best to cook for her and tease her to take her mind off her stressful work. When Leticia questioned her mother's motivations and wondered if she had any happy moments in her life, Sonia said, "Yes, when I come home and see all you."

Sonia was seen as a pioneer for being the first to bring the case of stateless Haitian-Dominicans successfully to international courts in 2005. She received such honors as Amnesty International's Human Rights Ginetta Sagan Award (2003), the Robert F. Kennedy Human Rights Award (2006), and the International Women of Courage Award (2010), presented by Michelle Obama and Hillary Clinton. In 2007, she was named one of the hundred most influential Dominican women, which earned her a public display in Santo Domingo that was vandalized and torn down on a daily basis because of her Haitian roots. She was soft-spoken but made her organization's mission poetically clear when we visited her office. MUDHA is fighting, she said, for Haitian-Dominican women to have two of the most basic human rights: a name and a nation.

MUDHA has been purposely kept small so it can avoid red tape and provide immediate help when needed. For example, MUDHA workers went to Haiti at three in the morning the day after the devastating earthquake in January 2010 to mobilize support and build a women's center.

The organization has four main areas of focus: education, health, human rights, and worker development. Its primary health concern is getting bateys potable water, electricity, latrines (many have none), and safe housing. It runs regular workshops on civilian rights, reproductive health, and self-esteem. It has also focused much time and energy on education in response to a change in government policy that requires Haitians who want to enter school to submit a document MUDHA claims doesn't exist. "We're fighting against a system that's telling us we don't exist—that we're invisible," said Rosalita, a former batey student.

Rosalita's batey teacher said her message to the government would be: "We don't want your money or our teachers to be paid or a breakfast program. We just want to be officially recognized." She added that she had fourteen- and fifteen-year-olds in her fourth-grade class because there are no options for stateless people past that grade.

Jenny Moron Reyes, who worked closely with Sonia Pierre, said the Dominican government saw MUDHA as Enemy Number One, mainly because, over the past few years, MUDHA has gotten 1,780 Haitian-Dominicans documented. It was also the first organization to get Haitian-Dominicans to protest publicly on a large scale (more than three thousand people) in front of the Supreme Court.

Since the 2010 earthquake, in which a staggering 316,000 Haitians died and one million were left homeless, there has been a population surge in Dominican bateys, with increases of 20 percent or more. Small bateys typically have around seventy-five families, medium ones 250, and large ones up to one thousand. Many of the inhabitants are shoeless and have severely calloused feet. The number of people who contract parasitic diseases from the simple lack of shoes is incalculable.

While strolling one of Santo Domingo's busiest streets, El Malecón, along a shore lined with wind-bent palm trees and tranquil wooden café huts with spectacular views of the Caribbean, our students spotted a white obelisk highlighted by two large red shoes, along with a zero and the words *niño descalzo*: zero barefoot children. At that time, the Dominican government was pledging to end the problem of shoeless children in the country. Two years later, we saw the same obelisk with a new design commemorating the Mirabal sisters. The "zero barefoot children" promise was never fulfilled, especially not on bateys.

Our first full day in Santo Domingo, or the "Old City," began with a light breakfast at an open-air restaurant with a cool sea breeze. As I took a seat next to my students, a light sun shower began, so I shared the common Dominican expression about how a witch had just gotten married. In addition to being conveniently located next to our hotel, the restaurant offered a smattering of tasty Dominican dishes. I ordered the *mangú* (mashed, boiled green plantains), garlic toast, and fresh papaya. I was very pleased that the orange juice accompanying my meal didn't have oatmeal in it, as had happened in the past. The mood over breakfast was a mixture of fatigue and excitement, which reminded me

The Dominican Experiment

of a comment Kevin made during his orientation back in the States: "Be prepared to be exhausted on this trip but also nourished."

While some people like to take a baby-steps approach to exploring a culture, Kevin is more of a "make every moment count" sort of guy. So, for our kickoff event, he had us travel to a batey. They are often located in the heart of sugarcane plantations, because it made economic sense not to have Haitians leave their working grounds, which would have cost the owners time and gasoline. Their rickety homes are assembled by friends or family, and typically large rocks are on the metal sheet roofs, next to pants drying in the sun, to prevent the metal from flying off and hurting someone. Upon seeing the setup, a student said, "I wonder what happens when it rains." I responded that since there is no plumbing, on rainy days human and animal waste from the nearby woods washes into dirt-floored homes and seeps into waterlogged beds—beds shared by three or more people, with sleep regularly interrupted by rats nibbling on young toes.

Our trip to the batey required going off the beaten path. Half of the twenty-minute ride was on the highway, and the rest was on a dirt road where our driver had to navigate around an assortment of bumps, ditches, and livestock. I watched the students' faces to see if any were put off by the fact that we were so far from our hotel and touristy areas, but the only looks of concern were from the parents. I hoped we wouldn't run into a random cockfight, as had happened in the past, or spot the carcass of a nearly identical tourist bus stranded over a weedy garden island. Having the students outside their comfort zones is one thing; having them fear for their safety is another.

I always get a little nervous during my visits to bateys because I have heard stories in which visitors and humanitarians like Peace Corps volunteers were not exactly welcomed with open arms. Some Haitian-Dominicans are wary of visitors, especially from abroad. Many people who visit the bateys do so more for a photo opportunity or a story to bring home than out of altruism, so the skepticism is understandable.

I will never forget my first time on a batey in 2007.[18] First, we visited a makeshift, one-room school run by a Peace Corps worker. It was an aged shanty but seemed sturdier than the average home on the batey. The day we visited, the students were mixing concrete to build another

---

[18] Kevin's first social justice tour, in 2007, was a mix of students and teachers.

room for their school. For a moment, I was transported back to the 1880s in Tuskegee, Alabama, and could envision Booker T. Washington spouting inspirational words to his post-Civil War students as they erected their school buildings during the day and went to class at night.

Two of the older teenage boys were focused on the masonry work, while eight younger students, no older than eleven, carried buckets of water on their heads to pour into the cement mix. The younger students had their shirts pulled over their heads to offer a little relief from the buckets and the sun. It was easily over one hundred degrees that day.

While half of the students did the physical labor, an older group attended a class led by the Peace Corps worker, Cebellis, a petite Latina from Texas who fit right in with the local fashion in her cartoonish "You Can Have My Brother" T-shirt. She gave us a quick overview of the school day, which is broken roughly in half. During the first part of the day, students learn the four major subjects, and during the second half they study various health issues, including hygiene, pregnancy, and STDs. Cebellis said the theme for this school year was "I choose my life," a powerful creed that I later incorporated into my classes back home.

Attendance is optional at the batey school, but students are rewarded with things like free breakfast. In the schoolroom was a container holding dozens of toothbrushes, individually numbered. It reminded me of the woman who teaches next door to me, who has a similar apparatus on her wall that holds thirty calculators.

If I had to sum up Kevin's mission for Friends Beyond Borders, it would be easier to explain what we are not. We aim not to be a charity organization but to be a solidarity group. We are not wallflowers or voyeurs, but we want to engage and understand the roots of the island's problems. We don't harbor a hero mind-set but try to bear witness and offer hope.

One of my roles in FBB is to help break down the walls among people from different cultures. When we first interacted with the batey students, both sides seemed apprehensive. But after one of my activities, when it is successful, connections are made. In a matter of minutes, something meaningful has been shared between two groups of strangers, and they cannot consider themselves strangers anymore. Just as a common tragedy builds bonds, so does completing a task together while partaking in a silly activity.

My experience with group dynamics dates back to 1994, when I began working with children as a summer camp counselor at the YMCA. It was at Camp Blue Sky, held at New Jersey's Echo Lake Park (renamed Goose Poop Park by my fifth-graders), that I stumbled across the notion that it's possible to play all day and make a respectable living out of it. It was fortunate that I worked at a summer camp before becoming a teacher, because it was there that I embraced the importance of fun and excitement in a child's upbringing. I wish more educators would start out on a similar path, so they could appreciate the wonder children possess before it is stripped away with barked orders that they "need to learn this for the state test."

We only had time for one quick activity at the batey, so I picked a bold one. Before we began, I explained my philosophy for group activities: challenge by choice. Participation is optional, and one may opt in or out at any time. Since the concept of the activity needed to be translated to the batey teens, I described it in the simplest terms. "This activity is called 'Break the Circle.' All of us are going to link arms, and a volunteer is going to step outside the circle and try to break in," I said. "The one breaking back in should do his best not to hurt anyone. Lastly, even though this is an activity that will force us to be close to one another, please do your best to respect others' personal space."

As everyone formed a circle, one obvious problem remained: the left half of the circle was American and the right half was Haitian-Dominican. I needed to mix the students up but in a playful way so as not to draw too much attention to it. The easiest method, akin to musical chairs, was to assign everybody one of four fruits, and when I called out the name of their fruit, they had to find a new spot. I did this three times, and then we locked arms to keep the first person out.

The activity seemed to be a hit. Right away, the students in the circle squeezed together as hard as they could to keep one of the Haitian-Dominican kids from breaking in. The laughs were instantaneous and continued long after the game had ended, as both their students and ours reenacted the highlights. When I do these activities, whether in the Dominican Republic or at home, I consider my job to be making memories. Kids today grow up way too fast, and often without goofy recollections. Without these childhood memories, they often become hardened or jaded and lack a more innocent, carefree time to fall back on when life gets chaotic.

Afterward, I asked if I could have five minutes to process the activity with the teens. Processing is almost as important as the activity itself. It solidifies the experience and allows people to express their emotions. The first topic that came up was discrimination. Some noticed that the game reflected how certain groups work together to keep others away—and enjoy doing so. Another topic was perseverance. Breaking into the circle was a difficult task and got tougher as the group adopted new strategies. At that point, some of those on the outside gave up, while others became more determined. A few teens said they felt uncomfortable trying to keep others out of the group. They empathized with a struggling peer and wanted to let him in. When the processing was complete, we moved on to a discussion about the Haitian-Dominican students' educational hurdles, led by Cebellis, and I felt that our interactions were more candid and the dialogue more sincere.

When the batey students' class time was up, Cebellis said they wanted to walk us to the highest point of the batey, where there is a far-reaching, 360-degree view of the community with mountains in the background. Kevin turned to us, and before he could open his mouth, we were grabbing our backpacks and heading for the door.

The sun assaulted us as we left the school. It was the hottest hour of the day, but we tried not to let that dampen what had been a magical affair thus far. Before we started the long walk up the hill, an elderly man in a torn shirt passed by with stalks of sugarcane, and Cebellis offered him some pesos so we could all have a taste. He lowered his load, drew his machete, and chopped pieces for everyone. Within seconds, all of us had the sweet juices dripping from our mouths. We continued walking, leaving a trail of spit-out pulp behind us that I hoped wouldn't attract any wild animals.

The climb was daunting, but we drank plenty of fluids and shared them with our escorts. The youngest batey students—those mixing cement and others shuffling around on pieces of tree bark as if they were skateboards—dropped what they were doing and joined us. One, who apparently had a thing for blonde hair, went around flicking a few of our girls' locks.

As we walked, most of the batey children took us by the hand. Even though we had already bonded with the group, this made the experience more poignant. Most of us acquiesced without a second thought. Others, like myself, revealed our oversized American ideas of personal space; I flinched when a young student grabbed my hand from behind. John was a handsome boy with surprisingly chiseled features for a ten-year-old. He had a prematurely receding hairline and a slightly distended belly, obvious signs of malnutrition that are commonly seen on the batey. He was wearing a tattered T-shirt and drooping shorts. He didn't smile much, but he didn't frown, either. He just seemed content to have found a companion for the day.

After a few minutes under the pounding sun, we passed an overgrown baseball field and spotted the batey's equivalent of a strip mall: a one-story cement structure with eight shops side by side. The stores had bright blue doors with matching wooden shades. They also had American and Canadian flags roughly painted on the façades to indicate that they welcomed our patronage. The structure looked recently built and well maintained. The roof was in surprisingly good condition. When the local adults saw us approaching from a distance, the doors swung open, and they started hanging handmade artworks outside. The crafts were constructed from everyday throwaways and leftovers, from vibrantly painted Caribbean scenes to intricate baskets woven by the calloused fingers of these virtuosos of the scrap heap. Cebellis was at the head of the procession with Kevin and asked if we wanted to stop. The group needed a break, so we hit the mall.

The first store I walked into was selling artwork cut from metal oil drums into animal shapes and ornately perforated by a hammer and nail. A fellow teacher pointed out a turtle, and I could not get my pesos out quickly enough. One tip I read in a travel book about the Caribbean is that you should always negotiate prices at street shops. It is expected, and, apparently, vendors lose respect for shoppers who don't. But in the face of extreme poverty for the first time in my life, I was so overwhelmed by new emotions from one minute to the next that haggling with a woman as her emaciated children stood nearby—a woman who probably wouldn't see another cluster of customers for several days, if not weeks—seemed wrong. Let me be judged. If it helps, later in the week I would haggle a street vendor from five hundred to one hundred pesos for a straw hat. He came off as a tad aggressive, so I felt more comfortable following suit.

As we continued our walk, we saw that our bus had pulled up near the shops. This was a thoughtful gesture that allowed us to jump back on if the heat was too much or the experience became overwhelming. I walked with John and tried to communicate a bit more in Spanish, but he remained expressionless. So far, he had revealed only his name, his age, and an interest in my water bottle. Moments later, a larger version of him came jogging by and tapped him on the shoulder. John automatically removed his flip-flops, and the guy, who I deduced was his brother, trotted off down the hill. John was barefoot for the remainder of our walk but seemed indifferent when we had to navigate muddy puddles.

We finally reached the top of the neighborhood, where many of the teachers had hoisted the local youths onto their shoulders. My attention was on a twelve-year-old who was reflecting light off a broken CD to gain a clearer view into crevices. Seeing her prompted me to reflect on our mission on the island: to see what others fail to see, and perhaps to shine a little light on forgotten places. The shade offered a welcome respite, and we all took in the magnificent panorama of green mountains, spying a donkey under a tree, kids on horseback, and healthy banana trees. Children had joined the group along the way, and our numbers had doubled since leaving the school. I find Americans quite entertaining when I am back home, so I am sure we were a great source of entertainment as we traversed their community.

While we were resting, a fellow teacher approached me and asked what I thought about the handholding by the youngest of the batey group. A few other adults overheard us and joined in. Some mentioned that their partners had asked for a few pesos, so they suspected that they held hands out of opportunism. But Kevin, who was nearby, said, "Actually, many of these kids are often hit by their parents and older relatives, and they have come to see white outsiders as affectionate individuals. This is a great topic to explore, and I'm curious to hear what everyone else in the group thinks." We would delve into that topic further at one of Kevin's after-dinner debriefings.

Soon we were walking back down to the school. I bade farewell to John, and he released my hand. He pointed to my digital watch, and I tried to tell him what time it was, but he gave me an empty stare. I lowered it so he could have a look. In response, he pointed at his own wrist, and I realized he wanted the watch, maybe as a memento or as something to bring home for his family. Remembering Kevin's request that we not offer handouts during site visits, I politely shook my head, and he gestured toward my water bottle. I handed it over, and after his first sip, a few friends rushed over to share.

I gave John a nod and a wave. Back on the bus, I quickly pulled up images of him on my camera. While scanning them, I overheard our teens: "They weren't miserable." "They don't see themselves as needing help." "I'm impressed with their sense of community."

We visited a few bateys on the 2010 trip and eventually returned to the first one I had encountered but to a different section of it. It seemed that outsiders with good intentions had created a divide. Most people in bateys, living on less than a dollar a day, can only afford home maintenance when it is an emergency. When a religious group came to offer a lottery for the newly built homes in the batey we visit most often, it was contingent on one thing: the complete rejection of Vodou. This offer forced Kevin to pick a side. He could either stay with the segment of the community who were sending their children to the one-room school run by the Peace Corps worker or keep his relationship with those who prefer not to accept handouts. If you know Kevin as well as I do, I doubt you could even call this a decision.

Having chosen to keep a connection with those batey residents who weren't willing to compromise their religious beliefs for a free house, Kevin received something unexpected: an invitation to a Vodou ceremony. Considering the history of secrecy among people who practice Vodou, I was quite surprised by the offer. I took it as a gesture of appreciation toward Kevin for staying true to the community over the years. This rare opportunity would solidify my argument about the unmatchable authenticity of bateys.

Brought from Africa and reconstructed in Haiti, Vodou, whose adherents worship one god who takes many forms, is a religion of resistance. When the French colonized Haiti (then known as Saint-Domingue and nicknamed the "Pearl of the Antilles" because it was the richest colony in the Caribbean) in 1664 and tried to jettison its culture to make the people more pliable, Haitians held on to what was dearest to them: their West African dance, music, and religion. The more the

French tried to force new religious figures and prayers on them, the more fervently the Haitians practiced Vodou, despite knowing it would cost them their lives if they were caught. Amid such intense oppression, it made sense that the Haitian Revolution began at a Vodou ceremony. And after witnessing Vodou firsthand, I can assure you that it is a beautiful celebration of culture and is nothing like Hollywood might lead you to believe.

Haitians, led by Toussaint L'Ouverture, Dutty Boukman, and Jean-Jacques Dessalines, defeated Napoleon's army in 1804. Haiti became the first slave nation to gain independence, and Vodou became a way for its people to celebrate and reinforce their newfound freedom. France retaliated by imposing harsh fines (around one hundred million gold francs) that would take more than a century to pay off, crippling Haiti and paving the way for others to take their turn strangling the nation. It is hard to believe that the superpowers of the world stood by after Haiti won the war, allowing the new nation to be punished for daring to break its shackles. It is policies and penalties like France's that have kept Haiti struggling for most of its existence.

On the day of the Vodou ceremony, as we neared the batey homes with the sun fading in the distance and the sky darkening from blue to purple, the students' faces again turned to shock as they spotted skeletal dogs and homes that were barely standing. They looked at one another as they began to understand that one can never become accustomed to seeing extreme poverty so close up. A few students went from being excited about taking pictures from the bus windows to no longer being able to look outside because the sights were taking such a toll.

During the bus ride, Kevin gave a quick overview of what to expect. "The word Vodou means spirit," he said. "When the French colonized the island, it was practiced by Haitians to maintain their African identity. If they were caught speaking their native language or practicing their religion, they could be killed. Music is used during the ceremony to invoke the spirits. The people act as horses, and the spirit enters them.[19] The type of music you will hear tonight is called gagá." A student's hand went up. "No, it has nothing to do with Lady Gaga." The student's hand went down.

---

[19] Vodou is said to be a religion of ecstasy, in which people allow their bodies to be possessed.

As our bus pulled into the community, we passed, not too far in the distance, the school from my first time on the island. I ached to go back there, but I didn't want to appear ungrateful to our hosts. The first few students stepped off the bus and moved with soft but anticipatory steps. Those who were my own students had been hearing about bateys from Kevin and me for years. "I can't believe I'm actually here," a wide-eyed student said giddily to another, grasping her arm.

The students who spoke Spanish were at a major advantage. Those who didn't walked alongside bilingual students to get a rough translation of what was going on. Right away, the students encountered homes that were even more dilapidated than the ones in our classroom photos. Many were so worn down that their frames and innards were exposed. Near two rows of homes sat a very familiar building, one the students had seen and heard about more than any other: Ramonsito's Vodou workshop.

I was more anxious than usual to see Ramonsito because, since the 2010 earthquake and the subsequent cholera outbreak in Haiti, there had been reports of superstitious people lynching Vodou priests because they believed their country was being punished for controversial religious practices.

The near side of the spiritual shack was made of green corrugated metal that showed major signs of wear. The right half was made of thick tree branches in a diagonal pattern. It appeared that this half served as a patio. Covering both sides overhead was corrugated metal in alternating slabs of brown over blue. The defining feature of the building was the artwork on the left side, featuring a queen similar to that from a deck of playing cards. She was a white woman wearing royal blue and a golden crown, holding a small being that I thought at first was a child but clearly had an adult's face. The small figure was dressed all in white and also wore a crown. It was holding a book while reaching out to the mother figure. Next to them was an intimidating skull and crossbones. (Years later, it still makes haunting appearances in my dreams.) The painting to the right of the queen was of a white man in a priest's outfit holding a wooden cross in his left hand and a skull in his right. A candle burned on top of the skull. At the far end was a white pitcher with a design that resembled a compass rose, accompanied by drawings of stars and one all-watching eye.

During a previous teachers' tour, we had arrived at the batey at an ideal moment. There wasn't much going on; Ramonsito, the "president of the music," was free, and an hour of daylight was left. Ramonsito is average height, with a buzz cut with four shaved lines in the sides and a bright smile that never falls from his face. Kevin, drawn as if in a trance, went directly over to greet him, exchanged a few words and bottles of rum, and said we could enter Ramonsito's personal hut as long as we touched nothing and didn't take our cameras out. Only a handful accepted the offer.

We teachers walked through the porch area, and Ramonsito held the door for us. The best way to describe the room is "dark"—not so much in color but in aura. Black symbols were on the walls, white plastic bags of unidentifiable substances were hanging from the ceiling, and playing cards were scattered on what appeared to be Ramonsito's work bench. While I have snuck my camera out in other countries, feigning ignorance, here I fought the urge out of respect, and a bit of fear.

Dr. Carrero of the Batey Relief Alliance said that when BRA was looking to study HIV/AIDS in the bateys, it reached out to this site. Knowing they couldn't just go in and take blood samples, the BRA leaders befriended Ramonsito and received a surprisingly quick yes to their request, on one condition. Ramonsito said they could take blood samples as long as Dr. Carrero shared the results and compared them with his. He performed his own tests, and according to BRA, they both identified the same people in the community who had HIV/AIDS.

Because of my past experiences at this batey, I expected our students to be stunned by Ramonsito's hut, and they seemed to be for a moment, until they noticed some welcome distractions. Two piglets sat underneath the painting of the intimidating priest, but they scooted away from the approaching crowd of students. There were also three agitated chickens on the roof of a nearby home, seeking refuge from the earlier rain. Several students took out their cameras to capture this peculiar sight.

Surprisingly, as day faded into night, the students grew comfortable with the unusual surroundings. One would later comment nostalgically on her evening at the batey, "I saw every star in the sky, like I was at a planetarium." After giving them some time to acclimate, we led them to the Vodou ceremony center, which Kevin called a ramada. It was made up of polka-dotted two-by-fours placed horizontally with slight gaps in between, and it was oddly inviting. Ramonsito escorted Kevin inside, our group trailing close behind.

The ceremony room was about the size of a standard classroom. Plastic chairs were set around the perimeter, and the students rushed to take their seats, with many vying for the real estate closest to the only door in case things took a wicked turn. CDs hung from the ceiling by strings, and to the delight of most members of our group, the ambience was more disco than Vodou for the time being. As I looked around I saw that, aside from Kevin and myself, everyone wore serious expressions that revealed their fight-or-flight mechanisms were kicking in. Kevin was smiling because we were experiencing something personal and extremely sacred. Perhaps he was also smiling because he knew that every single person in our group was staring at him for reassurance.

It was pitch dark outside. We were in an unfamiliar Vodou room, adjacent to a hut of mysterious practices, in the middle of a sugarcane field with stalks taller than us, a good ten minutes to the nearest paved road. If you stopped to think about it, we couldn't have been more vulnerable. Luckily, when things seemed to be getting tense, judging from the shuffling of people and furniture, Rich—who, at times like this, proves to be so much more than just Kevin's ground operator—wandered in with his arm around a batey teen. The sight of him allowed most of us to relax a bit.

More locals entered, about sixty in total now, greatly exceeding the room's normal capacity, and a few grabbed flags attached to long poles. One was the Haitian flag, but the others were homemade patchworks of various colors. Four older women held the flags and watched attentively as Ramonsito started placing objects around a thick tree in the middle of the room that shot straight through the roof. The tree was painted white and was adorned with a peculiar wooden tribal mask. Seated at the bottom was a life-size dummy with a stuffed monkey's head wrapped in green fabric. At the base of the tree Ramonsito placed several bowls containing white powders; one appeared to be flour, another cornmeal. Next, he lit about thirty thin candles around a large empty space in the middle of the floor. Music suddenly started pulsing and, on cue, the four women took their ceremonial flags and leaned them against the tree.

Ramonsito stepped out for a minute and came back wearing a ritual vest with white khakis and flip-flops. He grabbed one of the bowls and started sprinkling its contents within the empty space while his younger partner rang a bell near him. With the music quickening and the four women swaying at the tree, he started drawing a symbolic character in white—a *veve*, a five-foot-long image resembling the old cartoon character Captain Caveman—down to another tree painted white, which, upon closer inspection, was actually three smaller trees intertwined like snakes escaping through the roof. The music was getting louder, horns were thumping, young men were slapping their hands on tall, narrow red drums, and women were chanting. After drawing the *veve*, Ramonsito gathered what looked like coffee grains and placed a thin outline over the white substance. Two young girls assisted him. Soon the *veve* was complete and everyone stared agape at the otherworldly figure about to be summoned. It looked peaceful, or perhaps that was wishful thinking.

The music changed, and the women started circling the *veve* counterclockwise. Men with large, red metal horns and young girls in tight clothes joined the train as if powered by higher beings. The rotation around the *veve* is said to summon the channeled spirit. As the people were singing, dancing in a tight circle, and playing their instruments, I noticed that Ramonsito had lit a small fire on the floor at the feet of the monkey dummy. The fire stayed within the head of the *veve*. As the flames rose, Ramonsito grabbed the microphone and led his people in song. The horns, which resembled red PVC pipes of different lengths, became the main attraction. Each horn played one note, and the sweating men, who played their instruments with their mouths and a stick on the side, jammed along with one another as they circled.

At the climax of the ceremony, Ramonsito drew the four flag holders together, brought their poles to a point and let his whistle scream. With the flags gathered like an arrow, he carried them around the room. As the music played in hypnotic waves, he thrust the flags at each of us, releasing good energy upon us. (The faces in our group did not exactly express appreciation for his efforts.) After the flag holders made their way around the room, the music slowly died, and many in our group smiled, thinking the show was over—that is, until Ramonsito put his arm around Kevin. Kevin's face lit up, and he motioned for us to follow him out back, where a fire produced dancing shadows on the rooftops.

As we made our way around back, through patches of pitch-blackness, we were attracted to the distant, flickering light like moths to a flame. Turning the corner, we were welcomed by steady drumbeats, a bonfire, and festive Haitians still energized from the ceremony. The locals carried plastic chairs from the room and spread them over the rocky ground surrounding the fire. Ramonsito showed up but appeared to hand things off to a tall fellow in a saturated white T-shirt and a red bandana, who was holding his pet chicken.

Two of the younger men who had performed a tribal dance during the ceremony, wearing skirts composed of layers of shredded T-shirts, started things off with a slower dance around the fire. Others joined in, but the Chicken Man caught my attention. With the bird held firmly in his left hand, he grabbed a stick from the fire with his right. He blew out the fire at the tip and knelt down. Lowering the chicken to the ground, but maintaining a tight grasp, he appeared to pet it with the burnt stick, sliding the stick up and down its feathers. Judging from the looks of the locals, this bird was not his pet, nor would it see the end of the show.

Seeing me staring, our students shifted their attention toward the chicken. When the man was finished massaging it with the hot stick, he started doing a rhythmic dance around the circle. After a few minutes, he grabbed another stick from the fire, this time leaving it aflame. As he continued to dance, he occasionally swayed the chicken over the fire, and it frantically pulled up its legs. He did this a few more times, with the chicken becoming increasingly agitated. Soon, the Chicken Man's gestures were similar to those Ramonsito had made while dipping the flags toward us—an act to take away any bad energy we harbored.

After the Chicken Man had completed the circle and captured our and his people's negative flow, he grabbed the chicken's neck in his mouth, and the bird went haywire. Flapping its mangled mess of wings, it reached desperately with its claws for the Chicken Man's eyes. Behind the bird's frenzied efforts at liberation, the man wore a mischievous grin. Half of our students were on the edge of their seats, while the rest were covering their eyes with both hands. One student peeked up as the noise dissipated, not at the Chicken Man but at me, and I knew I had been caught with a huge grin. I felt a brief pang of guilt. I was enjoying this event not because the chicken was being brutalized, but because I had never seen anything like it in my life.

I broke eye contact with my student and returned to the spectacle in front of us. The chicken was still flailing about, trapped by the man's teeth. The entire episode, which lasted only two minutes but felt much longer, ended with what sounded like a person stepping on a twig. The chicken went limp. I heard a few students, or maybe adults, gasp. The man's dark eyes lit up, indicating that he was not done. He started swaying the chicken in our direction. He moved closer and stared right through each of us, the chicken dangling from his mouth. The students wore looks of disbelief, as did I, but we were experiencing opposite emotions.

This proved to be the end of the night's festivities, and several of our students walked away arm in arm. They appeared to be in a state of unspeakable shock, but they managed to find their way back to the bus. A few parents exchanged glances with me and Kevin, so I stepped to his defense, noting that on all our previous trips, there had never been a sacrifice. Their looks offered no encouragement. I hung by Kevin for a moment because he seemed to be having mixed feelings. He wanted the students to experience as much culture as possible, but he respects that there is a line and feared it had been crossed.

"I think they're just a bit shocked right now. It'll wear off," I said.

"I'm surprised they didn't squirt the chicken's blood all around," he replied. It certainly wasn't the response I was expecting, but I already saw him working mentally on how best to approach what we had witnessed when we got back to the hotel and had our debriefing. I asked if everything was cool, and he nodded.

We got everyone back on the bus after saying our good-byes and expressing our gratitude. Before the doors closed, several locals stuck their arms into the bus with trinkets to sell. They placed the goods in our hands and urged us to pass them around. We wound up purchasing a few beaded necklaces, small artworks, and an interesting bracelet ingeniously crafted from bottle caps. *Virtuosos of the scrap heap, creating something from nothing, necessity revealing a talent.* Once the sales were complete, we said our final good-byes. Kevin paused, microphone in hand, thinking it better to let things simmer a bit before we discussed the night's events. It was a wise choice.

On the way back I sat with Liz, one of our teens' mothers, who had hidden behind me during most of the outdoor ceremony. Fifteen minutes into the performance, she had grabbed my arm and said anxiously, "Michael, remember when you spoke about going outside our comfort zones on this trip? Well, it's happening now!" Safely on the bus and driving away from the batey, I figured it was a good time to see where she was at.

A psychological experiment once gauged people's happiness before a vacation, during vacation, and after vacation. The study found that people reported being least happy *while* on vacation. Keeping that in mind, on the occasions when things were taken to a higher level, I found it best to talk a good time afterward, when clearer hearts and minds could prevail. These conversations typically took place poolside at our hotel, and never once did a student, verbally or nonverbally, express that things had gone too far.

When I looked up at Liz, she noticed I was checking on her status. I could see that she hadn't found the right words, so I waited. She squinted a bit and threw me a curveball. "I really had no idea what to expect." Momentary pause. "We should do Vodou more often."

Liz was so moved by the student trip that she later signed up for one of Kevin's teacher tours. I chatted with Liz on her second go-around, and the remark that stood out most was about how her "priorities changed" when she got home. Not only was her teaching different, but her lifestyle was different as well. She added, as an aside, that she had already bought more souvenirs on her second trip because she had developed more of an appreciation for the island the longer she was there. On our farewell night of the teacher tour, Liz would tell the group, "It fed my soul to be with all of you."

It's a Dominican thing.

Chapter 4
EDUCATION IS NOT AN INDUSTRY; IT IS A RIGHT

Camaron que se duerme, se lo lleva la corriente.
(The shrimp that falls asleep is the one swept away by the current.)

Whenever I meet someone new after coming back from the Dominican Republic, the first question I inevitably get is, "Which resort did you stay at?" To me, that is so revealing. It's as if they are asking, "Since there's nothing else to do on the island aside from the sanitized activities orchestrated in some stuffy boardroom, which resort did you stay at?" The contests, musicals, and gimmicks they offer at resorts are as lame as the uplifting American '80s songs played as backdrop music while you eat in their unoriginally themed restaurants. Don't get me wrong, I love '80s music as much as the next guy who never threw out his mix tapes. But there's certainly a time and place for the things we love. Thinking you've experienced the Dominican Republic by staying at an all-inclusive resort is like believing you've seen California by visiting Disneyland.

Kevin often brings up the one show he saw while staying at a resort in the Dominican Republic. It was titled "Tribute to America" and drew quite a crowd of tourists. He tells this tale in a half-serious, half-joking manner, because when the performers first appeared on stage with the flags of both North and South American countries (all technically part of the Americas), the audience seemed at first confused, then hoodwinked, and several genuinely offended.

As stated earlier, I did choose to stay at a resort once, but my reasons were partly financial and foremost for research. Since I am antiresort, I figured I had to experience one so I wouldn't appear uninformed while bashing them. The hotel was near bankruptcy and offering rooms that were cheaper than anything nearby. Plus, they were throwing in three meals a day and unlimited drinks, which included a heavenly strawberry slushy that made my trek in the opposite direction of the beach well worth it.

So I stayed at an all-inclusive resort, and it was weak. I was off the premises nearly the entire day except for sleeping and eating the free food, which really wasn't bad. As I left the buffet one night, I noticed a wedding party, and the couple was having photographs taken. It made me think about how some people go into marriage realizing that it's messy at times and that there will be a fair number of headaches (which is why so many romance movies end at the wedding ceremony), while others approach it as the perfect diving board into a lifetime of constant delights. Needless to say, there was an extreme blandness to this couple's festivities, and I seriously doubted their professional cameraman was able to transcend the artificial atmosphere. The best I could wish them was that ignorance is bliss and that they live happily ever after in their fairy-tale world.

When my friend and I checked out in the resort lobby on our last day, I was sitting next to a group of women my age, and we got to talking. At one point in the conversation one of them blurted out in surprise, "You actually left?" I was about to ask her to repeat the question, but then it sank in—they had been inside the bubble for their entire seven days on the island, and all they had to show for it were their unimpressive tans. I was tempted to fabricate a story about how it was like a war zone outside the resort, but then I feared they wouldn't believe me afterward when I said I was joking and would take that story home with them.

The encounter left me wrestling with the question of why people travel to a faraway land just to be confined within secure walls. With that, why do so many travel magazines go to great lengths to highlight the top hotels around the world? Did you ever hear a friend actually say something like, "Have you ever visited Johannesburg? I hear they have amazing hotels!" One of my favorite quotes about people is, "The masses are asses." Trying to figure out people's motives is an uphill battle. That is not to say it isn't enjoyable to explore collective logic. The best I have come up with so far is that people like to be pampered. They like to be waited on and served drinks so that others will be convinced they are important. Actually, it's more likely an attempt to convince themselves that they are special enough to have servants.

If, by chance, you happen to be reading this book right now at a resort, let's just agree to disagree. My philosophy goes with the saying, "Ships are safest when in harbor, but that's not why they were built."

I'm an early bird, especially when in a foreign country, because I cannot bear to waste precious daylight hours. (Of course, my rejuvenating midday naps are an exception.) As often happens, I was the first to arrive at breakfast, and I got a little peeved when *desayuno* was advertised as being at a certain hour, and the lights hadn't even been turned on yet when I arrived. I quickly began to calculate the number of minutes of sleep I could have gained had the hotel workers been more punctual.

In this instance, I was pretty certain I had eaten there with several students at the same time the day before, but then I started to have doubts. Knowing that the American habits I haven't been able to shake often get me into awkward situations, I tried to figure out if this lateness of breakfast compared with the day before was just a Dominican thing. The only peculiarity in my recent memory was that the hallway near the elevators was soaked from a violent storm.

In fact, the previous night's Santo Domingo tempest had been so powerful that as we crossed the street, a rushing river that had formed along the curb stole two of our students' flip-flops and bobbed them up and down mockingly as it dragged them away. Our driver and Yunior went to great lengths to follow the water's course and locate the missing footwear. But after ten minutes of circling the Colonial Zone, which turned out to be a laugh a minute with the bizarre objects that masqueraded as the flip-flops, we had to declare it a lost cause, leaving the students to dine in one of the capital's fine restaurants, a popular locale for wedding parties, drenched and barefoot.[20]

After that wild water misadventure, Kevin shared his own Dominican flood story. (He seemed to save his best stories until we were on the island, perhaps so as not to scare away the timid.) The flood he recounted was more stagnant, but the prickly sensation he felt between his toes while wading with others through a busy street made it much more memorable: "The tail that slithered in and got tangled between the top part of my open-toed flip-flops belonged to the hairiest rat I've ever seen."

Waiting for breakfast the next morning, as the sun started to shine on the colorful buildings along the narrow street in front of our hotel, I walked through the automatic lobby doors and found all the nearby walkways desolate. There wasn't a single person in sight, and I felt discombobulated when I heard "Jingle Bell Rock," in July, from a distant radio. Figuring it best to give it a little time, I returned to the lobby, parked myself on a couch and engaged in one of my favorite travel pastimes—deleting weak photos. After trashing several dozen bad-angle shots, I saw the lights flicker on and a gentleman at the front desk shuffling some papers around. He glanced my way and went back to work. I got up to ask about the dining room, and he said that most of the staff hadn't arrived yet because of the flooding and that breakfast

---

[20] When I ask Dominicans now living in the States what they miss most about their country, many pick the downpours from their youth. They light up while reminiscing about grabbing soap and shampoo buckets, then running into the streets with their friends as they lathered up. Having witnessed the handstands, puddle splashing, and testing out of new dance moves under the most torrential of rains, I can say it is a sight to behold. Each time, I wonder if there's a connection between Mother Nature's showers and the Dominican birthday tradition of dumping water on the lucky person's head.

would be served shortly. Grudgingly, I sat back down and waited. My eyes got heavy after a few minutes, but just as the light started to fade, the elevator dinged. Four of our teens were staring at me with half-opened eyes. I relayed the bad news.

One of the running jokes of the trip arose each time our students asked Yunior how long it was until our next excursion. "Do you mean Dominican minutes or US minutes?" he would always respond. It would take some of our students a few days to embrace the carefree attitude on the island. "We don't follow schedules" is a remark often overheard there. Dominicans' lax mentality, similar to European views on the clock, must be contagious, because during the twelve days between the student and teacher tours, I managed to make the same misspelling on restaurant bills on back-to-back days, *of my own name*.

After we ate breakfast, we got on the bus, and even though there were scattered dry spots on the sidewalks, the main roads were still flooded, and the sewers seemed to be backed up. The newspaper ladies waved the morning issue of *Listín Diario*, the fruit vendors walked right up to our bus trying to make eye contact with potential buyers, and children in ragged clothes knocked on our windows while rubbing their bellies and pointing to their mouths. Attempting a shortcut, we passed some nice homes where broken bottles served as barbed wire atop uninviting cement walls, but in the end we wound up not much farther along than we had started. All motor vehicles were at the mercy of the impassive traffic cops.

The driver told us that our bus had a special bottom that could handle wading through a few feet of water, but given his sarcastic nature, we were slow to believe him. When Yunior nodded, though, we were reassured. A few students then asked about the attached luggage carrier, and Yunior replied that it shouldn't come off. When I looked at the students, whose passports, cameras, and other valuables were back there, their expressions told me they wanted to ask if the attachment was also fitted with one of those fancy waterproof apparatuses, but Yunior seemed to dismiss their question because the answer would make them more uneasy.

Driving in the Dominican Republic is an art. First off, stop signs and red lights are treated more as recommendations than as rules. This is especially so at night, when waiting in a stopped car can leave one vulnerable to *bandidos*. Driving on the wrong side of the street and seeing a man steer while his wife serves him beer from a brown bag both happen quite frequently and are, surprisingly, tolerated. When it comes to taxi drivers, there appears to be a custom that you must enjoy a beer with them at a roadside *colmado* (small grocery store) when you reach the halfway point to your destination.

That being said, I have to say that Dominicans are the most courteous and patient drivers I have encountered. It was mind-boggling to see a car drive the wrong way down an exit ramp and not one car honk in road rage. My only disappointment was the lack of helmets on motorcyclists, which is mainly an economic decision.[21] Kevin joked that it was easy to spot Peace Corps workers because they were the only motorcyclists wearing helmets; apparently, it is a strictly enforced policy for them.

Every day, I was shocked by how many people I saw missing limbs. At first I attributed it to violent fights, but Yunior corrected me, saying the overwhelming majority of the handicapped got that way from motor vehicle accidents. On one tour, a few teachers saw a motorcyclist crash into a car and were stunned at how long he was suspended in air before tumbling to the ground. The first time I saw a vehicle hit a pedestrian, within five minutes a dozen men with flip-cams were recording the aftermath, hoping to earn a nice buck from a television station. I would surreally witness the event again just a few hours later on the evening news.

Despite knowing how frenzied the streets in the Dominican Republic can be, I was still persuaded to take the wheel for a couple of hours when my wife needed a break on the way to Samaná, and on the way back to Santiago. With kids darting, motorcycles zipping, trucks looming, open manholes, and the edges of the streets crumbling away chunks at a time, driving there has the feel of a video game. I remember thinking, "Who needs to partake in off-road excursions here?" The streets offer more adventure than you can imagine, including the occasional vehicle on the wrong side of the road, heading straight at you.

On our early-morning bus ride, I took the opportunity to share spontaneous comments on the things we passed, using my best safari voice to make it entertaining. Before I spoke, I took in the energy from the street regulars: the guy with phone chargers hanging from his neck

---

[21] When helmets are worn by Dominicans, they are typically on the elbow because they are uncomfortable and make the riders sweat. Dominicans often tease friends recently in minor accidents by saying, "I think your elbow is going to be okay, but I'm not so sure about your head."

who also hawked cell phone minutes, the kids waving hard-shelled green citrus fruits called *limoncillo* that resemble bunches of grapes, the delivery guy leaning into a rusted wheelbarrow filled to the brim with yucca, and a money changer fanning his bills in the air and barking out his monosyllabic trademark, "Change!"

"Up ahead you will observe a woman walking with an umbrella, yet it is now sunny and no longer raining," I said. "Some say that when the sun is out, many Dominicans will use an umbrella not so much for protection from the sun's harmful rays, but so they don't become *too* dark and appear Haitian. Another anomaly you might notice this week is that on cloudy days many women will still be wearing sunglasses. They do this to avoid eye contact with men, who take the slightest sign as a level of romantic interest. Lastly, when rain is in the forecast, you will observe many young women wearing hairnets, something Mr. D'Amato finds extremely . . . appealing." This comment, made to determine how many students were listening, earned me a few hoots from the peanut gallery. "When the downpour begins, the hairnets are quickly and disappointingly covered by plastic grocery bags.

"To the right, we see a few men engaged in a chess match. Spectators enjoy the game played at a faster pace than we are used to seeing at home. More noticeable than sidewalk chess is dominos, a very loud and social game." One of the first photos of the Dominican Republic that Kevin ever showed me was of a guy playing dominos with his friends. He had several clothespins attached to his face and beard. While some play the game for money, others attach a painful apparatus to the face to make it just as enjoyable or even more so. I bet our school's chess club would double its roster if this twist were introduced.

"Lastly, on our right you will notice young children in blue dress shirts and beige khaki pants. These children are waiting to catch a ride to their public school. While public schools are technically free here, there are three fees, making it difficult for children to attend: registration, uniforms, and books."

The Dominican Republic is at the bottom of the list in Latin America when it comes to schooling, ranking near last for financial investment in students.[22] Half of its residents from ages fourteen to

---

[22] In recent years, according to UNICEF, the DR has budgeted 2.2 percent of its GDP for education, compared with Cuba's 13.1 percent.

eighteen don't attend school, and it is common to see fifty to seventy students in a classroom built for thirty-five. The school bathrooms are often in deplorable condition, and an estimated 70 percent of Dominican schools don't supply students with safe drinking water. Added to this frightening data is the fact that bateys are not included, so the actual numbers are much worse.

These statistics were provided to us during a teachers' tour by Maria Teresa Cabrera, the current, and first female, president of the Dominican Republic's national teachers' union (Asociación Dominicana de Profesores, or ADP). Cabrera, who was later elected to represent Latin America on the executive board of Education International, argues that the current education system in the Dominican Republic needs to change because it is "reproducing inequalities."

In 1992, there was a nationwide movement to address the country's educational issues by formulating a ten-year plan. One of the biggest shocks was that much of the language in the existing laws dated back to the 1910s and thus excluded a large number of the current population from the guarantee of education. Research also showed that many teachers were leaving the profession because their salaries only covered about 20 percent of their basic needs. Despite recent successes, Cabrera, a petite woman with ice water in her veins, said, teaching continues to be "an unattractive job to go into," with the average teacher making $250 a month.

After collecting data on the current conditions of schools, ADP designed a three-tier approach and took to the streets, hoping to compel the government to fulfill its promise (according to the DR's General Law of Education: Law 66-97, Article 197) to devote 4 percent of their GDP to education. The group's first step was to reach out and create a dialogue within individual communities. Second, it focused on spreading public awareness of educational issues through the artful display of photographs of typical school conditions. Lastly, the teachers and supporting activists set out to obtain one million signatures (in a country of ten million) in support of the 4 percent promise.

Once the three-tier approach was in place, ADP's campaign for a dignified educational system kicked off with a peaceful protest in December 2010 at the National Palace in Santo Domingo. Some say it was the largest public campaigning event in the country's history. Determined teachers used yellow umbrellas to protect themselves from the harsh sun. Unfortunately, while the umbrellas made up for the lack of shade, they did not shield the teachers from violent attacks by the police. These abuses were caught on film, prompting even more public support, from celebrity endorsements on television to Spaniards gathering in front of the Dominican embassy in Madrid. The attacks were widely considered barbaric, and the union created a day of solidarity known as Yellow Monday to show its strength in numbers. From the *motos* to the vendors, from the television announcers to that day's newspaper, it seemed all ranks of people were dressed in yellow. Ever since, teachers and activists have designated the fourth of each month at 4:00 p.m. as a time to stand up with their 4 percent umbrellas.

The campaign was successful, and the longstanding 4 percent promise was included in the country's 2013 budget. However, 65 percent of the education budget was earmarked for the construction of schools, specifically the building of ten thousand new classrooms, which Cabrera claims is not feasible in one year. "Teachers weren't a priority when they were allocating funds with the new budget," she said, adding, "We're doubtful they are actually going to spend the 4 percent."[23]

Cabrera ended her talk with us by arguing that standardized testing is "paving a path toward privatization" of schools in the Dominican Republic, shifting public tax dollars to corporations. She echoed what many of us public school teachers in the United States fear is the number one threat to our children's education: "All of a sudden the teacher is to blame for all the bad things that happen in education." She told us that education "should not be in the hands of any business," and spoke about the need for horizontal decision making. Just before she invited us to watch the animated public service announcement ADP had created in "Story of Stuff" style[24] to help with its campaign, Cabrera left us with a seed of empowerment: "Education is not an industry; it is a right."

Later, when I spoke in one of my classes about the Dominican school system, a Haitian student shared her educational memories from

---

[23] In an April 2014 email from Rich Weber, he wrote about "significant changes in the educational system at large over the past year," "gigantic new schools all over this country," people going to great lengths to "provide breakfast and snack to students," and that their efforts were "notable and impressive," but "this doesn't change the fact that the teachers aren't earning what they want/need/deserve."

[24] The ADP's public service announcement can be viewed at www.ceritoycruz.org

across the border. Sandra, who used to have to buy fabric and bring it to a seamstress to create her uniform, noted that Haiti has the lowest primary education enrollment rate in the Western Hemisphere and that more than half of children there receive no education because many of their families send them out to be servants. Despite all that, she said, schools are tightly run. "If you don't do your homework, you are suspended for a week, sometimes two," she said. "If you curse at a teacher, you get suspended for a month. If you get into a fight, the teacher or director beats you." Then her memories took an awkward turn: "Some girls sleep with their teachers to pass."

When I asked how much teachers earned in Haiti, Sandra said, "From $150 to $200."

I replied, "For a month?"

She shook her head. "A year." She ended by telling us that students caught speaking Creole instead of French were reprimanded and that the country's literacy rate was just barely above half.

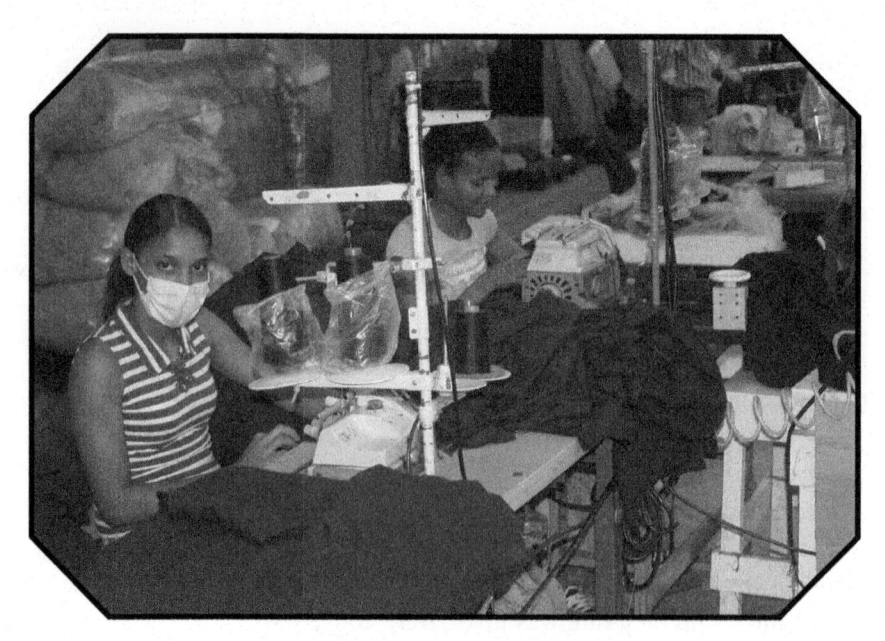

Workers at Alta Gracia

Chapter 5
THEY LISTED *PAPI CHULO* AS THEIR NUMBER ONE LIFE GOAL

Despues de la excusa, nadie queda mal.
(After the excuse, no one ever looks bad.)

When I taught world geography to seventh-graders, the first homework assignment I gave was to predict where their clothes were manufactured and then make a bar graph to display their actual findings. (Many of my assignments are cross-curricular in design because tasks tend to produce better results when students need to apply multiple areas of knowledge.) The day the clothing data was due, we would analyze their results through a series of questions. "First off, any surprises? What do your top three countries have in common? If you were going to build a clothing factory and wanted to be successful, where would you build it and why?"

The Dominican Experiment

A lot of what we are required to teach today is outside the average student's frame of reference and interest. But by connecting complex topics such as exploitation, fair trade, and unions to familiar ones such as candy bars, clothes, and coffee, teachers can quickly and smoothly build a bridge between a student's life and the rest of the world. After my students had established that it made sense for companies to build factories in developing countries because they could pay people less, pollute the environment without repercussions, and not worry about strikes, it was a small step to get them to see the value of a union or fair trade organization that fights for the rights of exploited workers.

On paper, unemployment in the Dominican Republic is around 15 percent. However, when we spoke with a few factory union leaders, the number they gave us was two times higher. The gray area between employed and unemployed is where *chiriperos* fall. Whether it's the paltry minimum wage,[25] the difficulty of obtaining identification, or simply the lack of jobs, many seek out intermittent work as day laborers. "Having no documents means being given a job as opposed to searching for one," Christal Earle of Live Different, a Canadian group that works to motivate young people, told us. "One in four children in the world is born without a birth certificate . . . and a birth certificate is a ticket to the future." She added that she sees her birth certificate as "my ticket to choose to do whatever I want to do with my life."

The question adults feel the greatest need to ask youth in developing countries is about their future occupations. When one of the parents on our trip asked some Dominican teens about their dream jobs, I expected to hear lofty aspirations to become baseball players, doctors, and lawyers, but I was way off. The young men laughed but appeared serious when they listed *papi chulo* (roughly translated as "pimp daddy") as their number one life goal.

That brings us to the term "doubly marginalized." The countless waterfalls and white sand beaches might paint a picture of paradise in the

---

[25] The minimum wage varies based on the type of work.

Dominican Republic, but most people there live a vulnerable existence, especially the women. Many young men sum up their ambitions by saying they want their wives to be the breadwinners—and after her full day at work, while he is at home or hanging with friends, the men expect their wives to bake that bread as well. That's a second shift of work, and we haven't even factored child-rearing into the equation.

The Dominican Republic is a machismo society. There are obvious double standards in the expectations of boys and of girls. Male teens are encouraged to go out and party late. Female teens are scolded by their mothers and told they look like *putas* (whores) if their clothing is too tight or revealing.[26] This double standard only grows as people get older. I am told it's typical for men to have a mistress or two. Many men live with one family but financially support two or three. Women, on the other hand, won't even tell their best friends if they are carrying on an affair because it is so taboo. Evidence of infidelity can be seen in the country's popular drive-in, "no-tell motels," where you pull into a nondescript garage and open the door to your pay-by-the-hour room.

Women have it tougher in most areas of Dominican life. This imbalance used to be particularly pronounced in the island's *fábricas* (factories), until unions stepped in. The first free trade zones (FTZs) in the Dominican Republic had no unions, and workers were beaten and spat upon. In the 1980s, the factory workforce was made up entirely of women, but an economic crisis forced men to start joining the garment industry. In the early 1990s, factory workers were flat-out prohibited to unionize. This was part of the country's sales pitch to lure companies to break ground there. "Multinational corporations were originally told there were no unions or rights to organize," thus making the Dominican Republic a very attractive place to do business, said Elizabeth,[27] the vice president of the Free Trade Workers Union. In 1992, workers tried to form the first FTZ union, but because of political corruption, its leaders "ended up in jail and suffered a great deal."

Even today, despite their major accomplishments, union leaders have to visit workers at home because it is too dangerous to recruit

---

[26] That news wasn't surprising to me, as it was pretty much the same when I took students to Italy.

[27] The following names used in this chapter were changed to protect their true identities: Elizabeth, Cristian, Patricia, and Johanna.

in public. "We go to homes, worker by worker, convincing them and educating them," Elizabeth said. "Rarely is it a one-time visit. Often, it takes up to ten visits before they sign up." Another union leader said it was common for factory bosses to use scare tactics and tell their employees, "If we see you even near a union organizer, you will be fired."

Elizabeth—wearing her hair up with sunglasses resting on her head, blue jeans, and an orange shirt with hearts announcing, "This Is What Love Looks Like"—told us that Article 47 of the Dominican Constitution gave workers the right to organize, but that private industries used a "propaganda campaign" to limit awareness of that right. "Workers have been misinformed here," she said. "They think union organizing is illegal, and they'll have to live in fear if they join. They think factory owners are more powerful than they really are."

When a student asked why Dominicans worked under such shady conditions[28], Elizabeth gave her honest opinion on factories in free trade zones, with each of her sentences spit out faster than the last, forcing our interpreter to grab her knee and slam on the brakes. "They come to countries like ours because people are desperate and willing to work for very little. Free trade zones are an evil need because people are willing to work for nothing and face oppression. It's a system that's designed to work them hard and leave them old, and the countries get rich off them." She added, "Many conditions here are similar to what you would find in Bangladesh."

Cristian, the secretary general of the Free Trade Workers Union, added, "It's not that there aren't good laws in the DR, it's that they are not being implemented. Plus, there are no repercussions to the businesses. Our constitution gives us those rights . . . but many threats were made against workers, and people were exiled." In the Dominican Republic, just like in the United States, politicians receive lots of money from the private sector, so they are not inclined to speak up for workers' rights. The union leaders tried reaching out to the companies, saying, "It is possible to have a union and have a successful business here." The corporations gave their standard reply: "If you unionize, we'll leave your country."

Soon after Cristian, a stocky man in blue jeans, a red polo shirt, and Nike sneakers, started to take a vocal position at the workplace,

---

[28] There are approximately two hundred thousand FTZ workers in the DR.

his superiors told him bluntly, "We're going to fire you because you complain too much." Outspoken leaders are immediately blacklisted, so those who are fired can never get another job in the industry. When Cristian became a leader, educating and organizing workers, tensions overflowed outside the workplace and "came down to a violent confrontation using arms. There was a shootout, and we were fired upon. One worker was hit, but survived," he said. "We went through a lot to get a collective bargaining agreement. I was imprisoned twice and taken from the factories by guards and police." His own friends even pulled him aside to warn him that if he didn't tone down his activism, he was "going to get killed." The warning was prophetic; shortly after, he was pulled from his bed late one night in what was fortunately just an act of intimidation.

Cristian shared this story while taking the union's recent collective bargaining agreement out of his pocket and passing it around with a proud smile. The first agreement was signed and the union made official in 1994. It's no wonder the leaders took it as "a gift from God."

To attract businesses to FTZs, countries take care of the logistical tasks like roads, electricity, and plumbing. Most factories are kept in decent condition, but that is more about creating a sterile environment so the merchandise is kept spotless than about workers' health or safety. In regular factories, workers are often denied overtime pay, and older people are pushed out early so the corporations don't have to support them in retirement.

The FTZ can be detrimental to the psyche of residents in close proximity because the areas are not created organically. Having the government build a strong infrastructure, seemingly overnight, only when it's profitable can feel like a slap in the face to those in nearby communities.

FTZs are tax havens for multinational companies and were designed to make it simpler and cheaper to ship merchandise across borders. During our tour of the Alta Gracia factory—which, like all FTZ factories, is fenced in and sheltered from tariffs and labor laws, but unlike other FTZ factories has a parking area with twenty-seven shining motorcycles—one poster stood out among the work-related memos tacked to a large, centrally located corkboard. It was in honor of Mauricio Báez, who was a popular labor organizer "during a time when there were many deaths for organizing," Cristian said. Báez became a martyr for the cause when he was executed for fighting against the exploitation of the workforce. A monument in his honor stands in Santo Domingo. The union leaders kept their comments about Báez short, perhaps because his death was too close to home.

Our conversation with Elizabeth and Cristian, along with a few workers in the union, was startling and filled with empowering stories. We prepared the students by having a few of them rehash factory situations around the world based on their research from class projects. The students mentioned that workers in Mexico, mainly women, are forced to work well after dark if they don't reach their quotas—"forced" meaning the doors are locked during overtime. (Overtime is probably a poor choice of words, because they are not usually compensated for the extra hours.) An immediate result of the extended shift is a late-night walk home, because buses don't run that late, and cabs are too expensive. Lots of women disappear; the police are suspected to be behind many of these abductions.

One student brought up the frequency of miscarriages among pregnant women working under such taxing conditions. With regard to why people work at these factories if the conditions are so deplorable: Just before the North American Free Trade Agreement was implemented, those who stood to profit most pushed to have the Mexican Constitution changed to eliminate the right to communal lands, and plots the workers had been farming and living on for generations were sold to corporations, leaving millions desperate for any work they could find and making migration to major cities inevitable. That seems to be a popular tactic around the world: change the laws about land ownership or raise taxes so people are forced to give up their property.

Before the first American occupation in 1916[29]—also referred to as an intervention or invasion, depending on which Dominican you ask—the DR relied on its sustainable agriculture, and there was practically no hunger. But as a result of globalization policies favoring big business, multinational corporations cleared farmlands and overplanted sugarcane, a foreign crop. While the sugarcane was being planted, barracks were built to hold the Haitians who were brought in as a cheap labor force, thus creating bateys.

---

[29] In Junot Díaz's book, *The Brief Wondrous Life of Oscar Wao*, he writes, "You didn't know we were occupied twice in the twentieth century? Don't worry, when you have kids they won't know the U.S. occupied Iraq either."

Many use the staggering number of people killed in the 2010 Haitian earthquake to point out the inhumanity of taking people's land and pushing and compressing them into major cities like Port-au-Prince, where the factories wear them down and leave them more vulnerable to major catastrophes.

Most people who end up taking low-wage factory jobs don't want them. They are "fully aware of the abuses that go on, but it's their last alternative," Elizabeth said. The animated clip "The Story of Stuff" recently became an Internet sensation because in twenty minutes, it hints at how multinational corporations sneakily acquire the agricultural lands in developing nations where people have been successfully farming and living for generations, forcing the countryside inhabitants to search for jobs in the city, where the cost of living is often five times higher.

When considering the low wages of a worker in a free trade zone, think about how quickly reality reduces her already minimal pay. First off, someone needs to take care of her kids for the nine or ten hours she is away from home. That costs a dollar or two. She also leaves a little money for the babysitter to make the kids' lunch. Transportation to and from work might cost a dollar. And unless she works at Alta Gracia, there are probably no water fountains, so she has to buy water and possibly a meal there. When all is said and done, at least half of her take-home pay has vanished.

When union leaders in the Dominican Republic learned about the plans for the experimental Alta Gracia factory, located a short ride north of Santo Domingo in Villa Altagracia, their first step was to ensure the implementation of a fair hiring process, because workers had always seen that area as "corruption central." It took two years to set up the factory, with many eyes observing. Since the host country doesn't benefit from intervening, only one watchdog group has been documenting Alta Gracia's course: the Worker Rights Consortium, an international organization.

A worker we spoke with, Patricia, said she was on the fence at first about joining the union, but in the end it seemed like a win-win scenario. When she worked at a different factory, where she was not part of a union, she said, "If you had to get a prescription, your weekly salary was gone. Homes, families, and marriages were destroyed because of the poor working conditions." Family breakdowns are common because jobs are often far away, and children are left alone or with nonfamily members. Unionization has allowed for "better education and better nutrition" for Patricia's children. "That was impossible before," she said. "We now enjoy peace at home and in the workplace." Another worker, Johanna, said that since she joined the union, her family had gained access to running water, electricity, and health care.

Union members at Alta Gracia "have a voice in the company's decision making," Patricia said proudly. Contrast that with the workers at a regular factory who, when rumors of organizing started circulating, were taken from their stations for the day and sent outside to pick up garbage under the hot sun as a reminder of what might happen if they unionized. Workers are often bribed with tens of thousands of pesos to stay away from FTZ unions and instead join "yellow unions," which then continue to give the workers money under the table to keep their numbers high.

The atmosphere in the room became tense when Elizabeth spoke about these "yellow unions," or union busters who operate with a divide-and-conquer mentality. These groups—the corporations' answer to unions—often make deals with the local police to intimidate and make life harder for labor leaders.

Kevin's scheduling of our FTZ visit couldn't have been more opportune, because the week before—on July 17, 2010—an article titled "Factory Defies Sweatshop Label, but Can It Thrive?" had appeared in the *New York Times*. It was about Alta Gracia, which opened in January 2010 as a result of pressure from college students back in the States, the Worker Rights Consortium, and the unrelenting work of union leaders in the Dominican Republic, whom Kevin invited to dinner for more conversation. At dinner, the workers thanked the students, telling them that "international pressure was key in getting this factory built."

To fully appreciate the model Alta Gracia factory—suitably named after the Virgin of Alta Gracia, the protector of all Dominicans—it helps to look first at the standard sweatshop on the island. On a previous teacher tour, Kevin invited two union leaders from outside the area to help give us a clearer picture of what unfolds on the premises. First off, because unemployment is so high, simple supply and demand should tell you that there is a strong desire for these jobs, even though the pay is less than a dollar an hour. That's because many people feel FTZs offer "the only consistent work available," Elizabeth said. This level of desperation invites more corruption. Oftentimes, female applicants are pressured for sexual favors to ensure they get a spot at a new factory. Another union worker said women were often told straight out by their bosses, "You've got to be nice to me if you want to get far in this company." The sexual harassment doesn't end there, and in many cases it gets worse. The terrible irony is that women aim for these factory jobs because, for many of them, there are very few alternatives other than working in the sex tourism industry.

Nowadays, 70 percent of factory workers in the Dominican Republic are women. One factory owner, whom I met by chance and chatted with while drifting in the ocean, said this was because women paid more attention to detail. He used the example of how men versus women shop. The woman picks up a garment, inspects the stitching, looks for dangling threads, and tugs here and there, he said; men pick it up, check the size, and leave. Critics of sweatshops say the real reason women are hired is that men are more likely to start fistfights with their bosses over the outrageous work conditions.

When I spoke to the owner, it was a couple of days after we had toured his factory. "What did you think?" he asked, as if he had been watching us the whole time we were there. Perhaps he had been. I was a bit surprised by his arrogance, but with such high demand for the jobs, I can see how one might lose sight of his own role in the exploitation of desperate workers.

I wanted to ask him if it was true that, at many FTZ factories, women are given pregnancy tests before being hired, that they are denied their required paid maternity leave, and that they have alarmingly high rates of miscarriage as a result of their long shifts on metal stools. I was tempted to strap him to a polygraph and ask if he had ever had a part in hiring yellow unions to intimidate and threaten the lives of fathers and mothers—*in their own homes*—who are just looking to stop the cycle of mistreatment so the next generation of workers can earn a respectable living wage instead of spending days in jail because they tried to organize a union and the local police, who get kickbacks, were also trying to make ends meet.

I would have loved to ask all of these things, but I knew the questions would have fallen on deaf ears. These owners are so mentally removed from the issues that it would have been a waste of my breath. "We don't force them to work," he said as I prepared to leave. "They can quit whenever they like, and someone else will gladly take their place tomorrow."

When I share this story back in my classroom, many students see and even agree with the owner's point of view, which I think is good, in a way. I pride myself on presenting both sides of a story. Many social studies teachers proclaim that they are unbiased and never insert their opinion. That claim of objectivity is ridiculous and impossible. We are all biased, and to think students aren't perceptive enough to figure out your stance on major issues by the stories you read, the anecdotes you tell, the films you show, or, better yet, the topics you never explore is absurd.

I feel that introducing both sides of a situation is the professional and, more important, the moral thing to do. These are young minds we are working with, and we have a major influence on how they turn out. Therefore, giving them the facts on both sides and having them take a stance based on class discussions of the critical-thinking questions introduced for each topic is always the best method.

When students ask if I think the owner is wrong for trying to make a profit using cheap but voluntary labor, I answer with a different question: "If you offer a man with a starving family to trade a finger for three months of groceries, would you expect him to do it?" When most say yes, he would obviously do it, I ask them why, and they always come up with the same answer: he is desperate. Taking advantage of desperate people to increase your profit margin is an unethical and inhuman thing to do, but people try to justify it every day. People will always oppress others if it means they can work less. That's why there are still tens of millions of slaves in the world.

When the topic of slavery came up during the student tour, Kevin offered a unique perspective. First, he took a step back and discussed how Columbus used slavery on the island to obtain more gold—rewards such as necklaces with a brass or copper token for those who made their quota, harsh punishments such as cutting off hands for those who didn't. He talked about how the Taíno (which translates as "Men of the good") drowned their own babies and committed suicide to avoid Columbus's slavery. From there, he explained how exploiting desperate people and having them work in subpar conditions is "new-age slavery." When all things are considered, it is actually a cheaper system than typical 1800s plantation slavery in the American South. "When you don't have to feed, house, or provide health care for your workforce, it costs significantly less today to keep a factory, farm, or plantation running than it did when you had to regularly invest in your slaves," Kevin said.

Timber from Columbus's main ship, the Santa Maria, was used to build the first fortress on the island, and Santo Domingo became the first city of the New World, producing the Americas' first castle, cathedral, and university. Santo Domingo would also go on to serve as the first seat of Spanish rule in the New World. At the time of Columbus's arrival on the island, there was an estimated one to three million indigenous people.[30] Fifty years later, as a result of harsh rule, there were a few hundred. After a hundred years, no living Taíno were left on the island, making it home to the first genocide in the New World. A few historians have even claimed that if you collected all the precious metals unjustly taken from Latin America since Columbus's arrival, you could build a bridge from there to Europe.

Elizabeth and Cristian were adamant about their basic expectations: "full compliance with health and safety standards, ergonomic chairs, and, most importantly, a living wage" of about 19,000 pesos ($475 US) a month, compared with the current monthly salary of approximately 6,000 pesos ($150 US) for most factory workers in the Dominican Republic doing the same type of garment work.

In order to create a union, more than 50 percent of the workforce must sign up. Union dues are thirty pesos a week.[31] At Alta Gracia, a progressive factory, 87 percent of the 134 workers have signed up for the union.

After Elizabeth took us around a regular factory, she had us compare it with Alta Gracia. The two factories looked similar, "but to the trained eye you'll notice major differences," she said, pointing out, for example, the fuse boxes with warning labels and the clearly marked emergency exits at Alta Gracia. She then showed us bulletins at both exits with the name and a photograph of the emergency evacuation leader on duty. Another observation she made was about the workers' old chairs,

---

[30] Indigenous people inhabited Hispaniola for at least five thousand years before Columbus arrived.

[31] At the time this book was published there were about forty pesos in one US dollar.

which had no cushions or backs. When the union leaders were at Alta Gracia and saw the new chairs coming in, they assumed they were for the bosses, but after several dozen rolled through the door, they started wondering how many bosses they were going to have there. Incidentally, the workers at Alta Gracia have no bosses or supervisors, just instructors.

During our talk, the workers often made reference to the *canasta familiar* or "family basket," their expression for a living wage or dignified salary taking into account the average family's costs of education, food, health care, and housing. "A lot of time and studying went into what a family of five could consider a livable wage," Elizabeth said. Their *canasta familiar* estimate is 20,000 pesos a month ($500), three times higher than their current minimum wage. The union has also won the right to a "thirteenth salary," which is an extra month's pay given right before school starts, and it is working on getting a "fourteenth salary" before Christmas.

These union victories "don't just mean better treatment or fairness, but pride because they (the companies) follow DR and international law," Cristian said. Workers who previously had sleepless nights because they feared for their jobs and safety now say, "We've found a sense of security and peace."

Yenny Perez, an inspector of clothes, and the worker who came on our bus to give us a welcome before the tour, said Alta Gracia "was born out of a harsh struggle." But the hard work has paid off; "many workers at Alta Gracia say they feel like they're at home." She added, "We want to set an example for all the other factories in terms of being respected as workers."

Another worker we met said that he was often asked how Alta Gracia became so successful, and that he responded, "It didn't just fall from the sky . . . Many horrible things happened in order for it to exist."

Alta Gracia employees work forty-eight hours a week, Monday through Friday. Four days a week, they start at 7:00 a.m. and finish at 5:30 p.m., with two breaks: 9:00 to 9:30 a.m. for breakfast and 12:00 to 1:00 p.m. for lunch. On Fridays they get out at 1:00 p.m. They receive three weeks of paid vacation in December if they have been working in the industry for at least two years. If they have been working in the FTZ for five years, they receive two additional days of paid vacation, in accordance with Dominican law. Working on holidays is optional, and those who choose to do so are paid double time. Overtime work results in 30 percent more pay. Also, following Dominican law—which the factory did not do before becoming the world's first fair trade textile factory in a free trade zone—women receive three months' paid maternity leave. For good measure, Alta Gracia also throws in a basket of basic supplies after a woman gives birth and offers new mothers an hour each day to feed their children.

"We have really good health care," Johanna said. "We have the freedom to choose the insurance we will have. Before, there was no choice. We can include our whole family in our health care, including parents over sixty and 'husbands,' even when not married." Alta Gracia also takes pride in educating employees with frequent workshops on topics such as budgeting, business, economics, ergonomics, finances, and safety. "At the end," she said, "they'll each receive a certificate of completion that can help strengthen their résumés to help build a long-term career."

When asked about the work environment, Johanna said, "We all get along well." She mentioned that both Dominicans and Haitians work in the factory. A union office is inside the factory, next to the human resources office. Alta Gracia has a health and safety committee on site as well as a doctor. With such a dignified setup, it's no wonder the factory has more of a club atmosphere than a work one. The music is loud, or "bumping," as a student would later correct me; many sing along, and when the workers meet a quota before their target time, loud cheers spill out of the doors and into the nearby community.

The movement to open living-wage factories such as Alta Gracia was ignited by college students in the United States. When, under the banner of United Students Against Sweatshops, they first contacted their colleges' leaders about the source of school merchandise, the suppliers flat-out refused to say where the factories were located. The students then embarrassed university leaders, saying they "didn't want their university names on shirts made from slave labor." Shortly after that statement began circulating, a change in policy began. At last count, more than three hundred college campuses carried Alta Gracia clothing, mainly through Barnes & Noble stores. Alta Gracia is also said to be near a contract with Walmart, which I'm guessing is good news.

Alta Gracia's Facebook page states, "The concept of a living wage is straightforward: it means paying workers enough so they can provide their families with food, clean water, clothing, housing, energy, transportation, child care, education, and health care."

The labor leaders' and workers' main message to our students was inspirational. After one college student asked what we could do back home, Elizabeth reminded us that there's "nothing else like Alta Gracia in the world. Every success we've had has come at great risk. Take our message and spread it. Let the world know what's happening here. It's up to the consumer to demand that the products they buy are made in the right factories." She paused and looked at the student who had posed the question. "Find out the true owners of the corporations," she said. An Alta Gracia worker chimed in, "Our future is in your hands." It was surreal to see hardworking adults pleading with our teenagers.

When we were given this rare opportunity to sit down with the labor leaders, they spoke more passionately and directly with our students than with the adults. It felt as though they were speaking with their own children. Maybe they hadn't found the right words to do that yet, or maybe their children were too young to understand why their parents were risking so much for what some feel is an unwinnable battle. Elizabeth ended her talk by saying she was "grateful to the students for taking a break from the beach to hear our story." One student asked the workers what the biggest difference was for them now that they were working at Alta Gracia. Patricia responded, "The difference is between living in a home with a dirt floor and a concrete one, and that is the difference from being on the ground and in the sky."

Less than a year after the Alta Gracia factory was established, we were told by a woman who works for the Worker Rights Consortium, whose job is to visit free trade zones to make sure codes of conduct are being followed, that the children in the community already had new aspirations: to work at the Knights Apparel (the South Carolina-based company that created the Alta Gracia label) factory. It was so nice to hear loftier aspirations than wanting to be a *papi chulo*. These children wanted to work with dignity. Even the local motorcyclists were happy, because their profits had skyrocketed as a result of the increase in regular commuters. Compare those feelings to the ones of the people who felt "like the community died" when the company before Alta Gracia closed down.

When we visited in 2010, we were told that Alta Gracia was intended to be a one- or two-year pilot program and that the results would be studied around the world. At the time of this book's publication in

2014, it appeared stronger than ever. I get emotional each time I see one of the regular Facebook posts of success with those familiar faces.

One of Alta Gracia's biggest victories has been earning the contracts to produce the University of Notre Dame's "The Shirt" in 2012 and 2013. When I asked a worker why those two contracts were so significant, she said that one purchase in 2013, for 180,000 shirts, had generated three months of steady work.

While I did my best during our trip to thank the people who took the time to meet and tour the factory with our students, and to extend my admiration for the risks they were taking, the ideal way to express my appreciation for the Alta Gracia workers was obvious. When I returned to the States, I went to a college's website (I didn't choose my alma mater, but rather one with a turtle as its mascot) and ordered a hooded sweatshirt with the Alta Gracia label. The price was exactly the same as that of the name brands made in sweatshop conditions, and I felt hopeful that this endeavor might just work.

When I received the sweatshirt, I was very impressed with its quality and noticed a picture tag dangling from the sleeve with a small biography of Pablo Tolentino, one of the workers I had spoken with at the factory. Next to his picture were the words, "My son goes to school because of these clothes." *Using testimonials from workers instead of overpaid athletes to sell clothes—could that work?* When I opened the tag, his story continued.

> We live in Villa Altagracia, the town the company is named for. No company has ever cared about our community, but now we've seen that this company respects our rights. It's changing our lives. They understand how to work with our union. Before, we all suffered from unemployment—but Alta Gracia for us means hope. Alta Gracia makes a huge difference in the quality of life, and not just for me, but for my wife, son, and my mother. We make a living wage now, so we have the security to know we can make our rent every month, send our kids to school, and eat well. With each purchase, you are supporting a better life for our entire community.

Other tags contained similar comments. "It gives us the chance for a better education—even for me to go back to school!" said Mariza Vargas. "We want you to feel comfortable wearing Alta Gracia clothes, knowing they were made in a unique factory where the workers have united to form a union," said Yenny Perez. "With a living wage, I know I can afford to go to the doctor and get medicine when my family is sick," said Yolanda Simon. "There were times in the past that my children went to school without anything to eat, but now it's another story," said Manuel Guzman. And on the inside of the sweatshirt I purchased, where it lists the size, were words summing up the workers' sentiments: "Made proudly in the Dominican Republic."

This brings us to the official "Page 81 Challenge." I am humbly requesting, on behalf of my friends from the factory, that one of your next gift purchases be a fair trade or Alta Gracia product. Give a present that raises consciousness, and I bet you'll do it again within a year. *Your dollar is your vote.* Help put food on the tables of these hardworking, risk-taking people.

After our tour of the factory, where two of our teens spied their own St. Joseph's University sweatshirts being stitched and referred to it as a "home-run moment," Kevin decided to have our first debriefing at the factory while the information and emotions were fresh. (So far, every college student who has gone on our trip has found that his or her school sells apparel made by Alta Gracia.) Olivia got things going. "At first I was complaining about how hot it was. Then I realized this is what a good job in the DR looks like," she said. The response that received the loudest applause was Kalim's: "What really stood out is the attitude of the people we met. It made me realize how much Americans complain."

The comment that moved me most, though, was a simple thought: "I was surprised to see how happy they were." Before my first trip to the island on Kevin's social justice tour, I read a lot from the list he sent out and drew a picture in my mind of forlorn people. Being supersensitive, I feared that their sadness would overwhelm me. Then came the curveball: everyone I met was genuinely happy. Perhaps it's not what you have in your hands, but what you have in your heart.

On the way back to the bus, an adult asked Kevin how he thought the tour of Alta Gracia had gone. He smiled slightly and said, "I would like them to walk away with one question in mind: 'If this is fair trade, what is everything else?'"

Before we left the fenced-in free trade zone[32], an armed guard stopped our bus. He did a quick, brusque search and sent us on our way. We had our passports ready—Kevin had reminded us earlier that we were technically leaving the country—but the guard just wanted to make sure we weren't taking any of the apparel with us. The multinational corporations' interests are very well protected.

Surprisingly, in the Dominican Republic, items made domestically cost more than imports, with the exception of homegrown food. With imports, there is just one trip: from the manufacturing country to the DR. But items made in FTZs can't be sold inside the country unless they are shipped back. Yes, because international trade laws are designed to favor companies over countries, products "made in the Dominican Republic" have to make two trips to be sold in the Dominican Republic. They first have to leave, and then come back.

As we left the free trade zone and discussed the topic of imports with a few students, people were selling scraps of material sewn into decorations like Dominican flags. Apparently, people were hitting the trash bins and, like those we met in the batey, making art with what had been discarded nearby. *Virtuosos of the scrap heap, creating something from nothing, necessity revealing a talent, one's talents building an identity, pride coming from within.* The one I bought now hangs in my classroom.

---

[32] Alta Gracia is not the only factory in this particular FTZ.

Sosúa garbage dump

Chapter 6
THOSE PEOPLE YOU MET AREN'T MY REAL PARENTS, AND THEY BEAT ME

Se salió del tiesto.
(Getting out of your pot; acting more lively than usual.)

Before the student trip, Kevin emailed an itinerary to the teenagers and their families, as well as to me. I could barely contain myself while I waited for the attachment to download, with visions of bateys, beaches, white-water rafting, zip-lining, and of course, *tres golpes* (the breakfast of "three hits:" eggs, salami, and white cheese—typically served with *mangú*) dancing in my mind. But as I scanned the list, I kept getting snagged on one destination: *garbage dump?* I was wondering if (and part of me was hoping that) this might be a Dominican expression I wasn't familiar with—like the car wash, which often converts into a nightclub with live music until about four in the morning. By making these sites multipurpose, the owners rake in money during the day and night and cleverly save by only needing to pay for one license.

Truth be told, this would not be the first time I encountered garbage on a large scale. During my adolescence, I had the good fortune of living adjacent to a wooded area. While traversing our own secret jungle, mindful of the garter snakes that would flatten out right before an attack and the beer cans with drunken slugs hidden within, my friends and I would eventually reach our tantalizing destination—a half-abandoned industrial complex. For some reason, probably fear of our parents, we did not venture inside the buildings as much as we took advantage of what would become our teenage battleground: twenty-five-foot-long Dumpsters. *Who needs playgrounds when you have enormous Dumpsters?*

To this day, I cannot tell you if our parents knew about these adventures. We were too thrilled to restrain talk of our conquests to amid the rubbish, but the adults probably assumed we were talking in code or letting our imaginations get the better of us. What I can tell you is that the waste in which we cavorted was much safer than the trash compactor Luke Skywalker and Chewbacca navigated while rescuing Princess Leia. The main contents were thick cardboard rolls (which made for excellent swords and spears), romance novels with torn-off covers, and what looked like popcorn covered in paint. Surprisingly, our frequent visits left us unscathed. Somewhere in the back of my mind, I hoped our students would walk away from their garbage experience with similarly fond memories, but I also suspected they would be faced with much more interesting junk than my buddies and I encountered in our youthful days on the border of Linden and Rahway, New Jersey.

When our day at the Sosúa dump was finally upon us, there were a few whispers among the teens, as well as among some adults, about backing out. A number of students complained of sudden stomachaches during breakfast. In the end, though, everyone boarded the bus. I think they had been waiting for a brave soul to step forward and ask about staying at the hotel. Hopefully, their acquiescence was more based on trust in Kevin, whose trip had so far been nothing short of spectacular.

Our schedule that bright morning first required us to pick up Christal Earle, an attractive blonde Canadian with a plumeria flower tattoo. She is a motivational speaker and the cofounder of Live Different, "a movement about passion and compassion in action," which brings a music group to high schools to get teens excited about service learning. She would help us enter the dump, since the government is wary of outsiders seeing the conditions many Haitians work in to make a dollar a day. In addition to working with people struggling in the Dominican Republic, Christal also organizes trips to Haiti, Mexico, and Thailand.[33] She is an oratorical genius, and the way she energized the students ahead of the dump visit, which she referred to as an "in their shoes" experience, was astonishing. After informing them that "there's an incredible purpose for your life," she went on to say, "Something beautiful happens when those of us who have tools work alongside those who don't."

Christal's connection to the dump is special in that—aside from the powerful friendships she has made with the workers there over the years, about 90 percent of whom are stateless—the dump is how she met her daughter. She adopted the five-year-old with the beautiful braids and sunshine smile after her biological mother, a dump worker, died. "They are no longer numbers, but people I count as friends," she said of the workers, "and now, actually, many are family."

Christal then discussed a few themes to consider during the coming experience: the difference between compassion and pity, how silence is consent, and how understanding others breaks down our judgments of them. In the fifteen minutes she spent with us before we reached the dump, to which she has been bringing teens since 2005, she explained that the people there realize they have the worst job in the country and that they live in a place (a batey) that many people pretend doesn't exist, and in a country where they are not welcome. "Their skin is the wrong color, and they speak the wrong language," she said. We often talk in my classes about how Mexicans in the United States are needed but not wanted, so I felt confident my students grasped what she was saying.

Some of the people working there would be around my students' age. Nearly all of them walk the few miles to work, and some would be shoeless. "Some were slaves, and some still are," Christal said. Many Haitian children living in the Dominican Republic are restaveks, a French word meaning "one who stays with." (According to UNICEF, there are an estimated 225,000 to 300,000 restaveks in the Dominican Republic and Haiti.) Parents who don't have the means to raise their

---

[33] To learn more about Christal's work around the world, check out her website at www.yourbrillianceunlimited.com

children will send them to be domestic helpers, but all too often the parents are deceived—they are told their children will be doing "light work," but the kids wind up laboring in dangerous conditions and being abused. Aside from working in the dump, many restaveks in the Dominican Republic are shoeshine kids, sell candy from tubs on their heads, or clean up at barbershops. When Christal was in Port-au-Prince and glanced out her window one night, she was shocked at the number of restaveks sleeping on their masters' roofs.

This story of the poor owning the poorer clearly upset the students, so Christal assured them that the teens at the dump "really enjoy the fact that we work with them. Our message by helping is that we believe in you, and you deserve dignity."

Before we arrived, we picked up a Haitian worker with a glowing smile who taught us a few Creole phrases so we could better communicate with the workers. "The answer to the question '*Sak pasé?*' is '*Nap boulé.*' It's like you are asking how they are, and they are telling you they are good," he said. "The literal answer is, 'I'm burning up.' Everybody say '*Sak pasé?*' and then '*Nap boulé.*'" His energy was contagious, and the students enjoyed practicing the phrases. He noted that, while the English language has more than two hundred thousand words, Creole has about four thousand[34], so the workers may seem to speak quite directly and even aggressively. For example, it's common to hear assertive comments like, "I want that!" On a teacher tour, one worker called out to an African-American principal in our group, *"Morena, dame agua!"* In English, that translates roughly as, "Dark-skinned woman, give me water!" But on the island, *morena* tends to be used affectionately. Judge slowly.

After Christal's emotional talk, which she concluded by saying that she, too, would work in a dump if it meant a better life for her daughter, she explained that we would be paired up and that the workers were looking to fill their fifty-five-gallon trash bags—which could have easily fit my whole six feet two body—with plastic bottles, preferably crushed ones without too much mud on them. They earn twenty pesos (about fifty cents) a bag, and on a good day they will fill two bags. In a month, they earn about 1,000 pesos ($25).

---

[34] These numbers are debatable.

The Dominican Republic doesn't have a formal recycling program; instead, a private company buys the aluminum, glass, and plastics from the workers. Anywhere from twenty to one hundred people work at the dump on a typical day, but sometimes they aren't allowed in, or the garbage trucks don't come. The workers are often Haitians who, with their children, crossed the border illegally and trekked through backwoods to avoid military checkpoints. (The other option is to try your luck with the underground racket of illegal border crossing, but that is very risky.) When Christal asked them how they survived the journey, one responded, "People helped me. Everyone. Haitians and Dominicans."

Christal mentioned that before our hour and a half in the dump was up, the workers would likely ask for our sneakers, hats, gloves, and more. Her final note was a request that we remove our sunglasses, which she felt would create a barrier between the workers and us. The only person in shades would be the military guy in blue fatigues. We passed the guarded entrance, and the bus made its way up a dirt hill lined with shriveled tires. That was when my nose started to itch; just seconds later, I noticed plumes of smoke in the distance. After a bumpy two minutes, we reached the dump, which was larger than a football field, and looked like the remnants of a recent aerial strike.

As we prepared to get off, Christal reminded the students that the bus would be there, with water, if they needed a little rest or air-conditioning. With that, we put on our final applications of sunscreen, donned our worker's gloves, and opened the door. Before we could step out into the sweltering heat, we were hit by a one-two punch in the form of a cloud of flies and the stench of spoilage.

Before I got up, I studied the view from my window: three women relaxing and one man reading a newspaper in one of the few spots of shade, several shirtless men wearing nonmatching rubber boots with sweat glistening on their muscular frames, a mountain of cardboard into which a few of the younger workers were taking turns tossing one another, a frail man dragging a train of dozens of bleach and detergent bottles tied together, two guys wearing wool caps, and a luckier one in a bizarre tricorner hat, to protect their heads from the sun.

Before my second foot touched the dirt, a fly went right up my nose. I jerked back. Before I could tell if it was gone, one was in my ear and another on my lip. I fought the urge to turn around and get back on the bus. That's when I heard one of my students say, "I've never seen so many flies," and I thought to myself that perhaps this was why people covered their mouths when they yawned.

The workers quickly gathered to welcome us, and we had no choice but to take in the tangy fecal smell. They eagerly offered partnerships and went off to work with the most intrepid of our group. Each student started walking toward the endless mounds of garbage, gripping one end of a black bag while their coworker held the other. A few were overwhelmed by the heat and the vastness of the place. For those who needed help with introductions, Christal's motherliness took over.

As the students were partnering up, I saw a few men in flip-flops and open-toed sandals using long sticks to move around smoking piles of trash, one of which was still aflame. My attention then shifted to a truck carrying human waste to be dumped nearby. But before I had time to freak out about the waste truck, I noticed a section off to the side with folded clothes spread neatly over a blanket. A few teenage boys browsed the gently used clothes; one tried on a gray striped shirt that fit him well, while the other playfully put on a dress over his clothes.

As I was coaxing some students forward with motivational words and a reassuring smile, a tall twenty-year-old with dreadlocks greeted me. His name was Joelle, and I attempted a little recently learned Creole. He smiled at my feeble effort and asked if I spoke Spanish. A little, I said. He asked if I had a partner yet, and I shook my head. He smiled, put his hand on my shoulder, and guided me toward the sea of trash. When he learned my name, he was quick to rename me Michael Jackson, and we shared a laugh. I figured he was taking part in the Dominican tradition wherein people call their friends by nicknames so any evil directed their way won't be able to find its target.[35]

During our time together, we talked more than we picked up trash. Joelle seemed to long for someone to whom he could describe the plight of his people. I listened and tried to fathom the complexity of his life. He pointed to an attractive woman in the distance, likely his wife. I

---

[35] It's a comical moment each time my *media naranja* (half of an orange or "better half"), who is Dominican (yes, I wound up falling in love with more than just the culture), is surprised when she discovers the actual name of an uncle through a Facebook request, being that she has only ever known each of her *tíos* by their nicknames.

nodded toward her, and she smiled. Then, in Spanish, he said three sentences that will always ring in my ears: "This is where I work every day. I am very hungry. Please remember me." He repeated that last line slowly. As his words sank in, the best I could do was touch his shoulder. Then I motioned toward the bus and surreptitiously handed him a bag of fruit, trying not to draw attention. I had done well up until that point in following Kevin's recommendation that we not give handouts or money because the strong push aside the weak, hurting bodies and feelings. But that day I caved, mainly because Christal had opened the door slightly before we met our partners.

We talked a bit more, taking advantage of the shade cast by the bus, and then I told him I really needed to check on my students. We shook hands, staring into each other's eyes for a prolonged moment. Joelle walked over to his wife and handed her the bag of fruit. On my two subsequent trips to the dump, he was nowhere to be found. I considered inquiring but thought better of it.

I was happy to learn that there is a lot of turnover at the dump from year to year. Perhaps the sneakers, hats, gloves, and pesos hidden within the good-bye handshakes help some workers earn more than their counterparts, eventually allowing them to reach their goal: to return to Haiti with some extra cash for expenses such as school fees. If they are capitalizing on people's guilt, I see no problem with that.

Before I headed back toward the students, I noticed that our translator was on the bus, having lasted less than five minutes in the dump. "This is too much," she said. "Mentally, I thought I was ready." All I could do was put my arm around her and offer some water. Later in the week, she would express how grateful she was to be a part of Kevin's tour and tell us the trip to the dump had been monumental, especially because she was able to experience it with her daughter. "I never visited any of the places we saw on the trip, and I was born here and return almost every year," she said. Soon after I left her, I looked back and noticed she was giving it another go—this time working with our bus driver in his dress pants, polished shoes, long-sleeve shirt, and tie. Both our teens and theirs were left speechless.

Another garbage truck rolled in, and the workers raced over. They rummaged systematically through the new trash, throwing plastics behind themselves in a separate stash before putting it in bags. At first, several students would take from other piles to give to their partner, but honesty prevailed, and the students quickly learned the workers' system as well as their code.

A few of the youngest workers seemed less interested in filling their bags than in picking up plastic bottles and drinking the sip left behind, or reaching into large tortilla and potato chip bags and scraping the bottom and sides for any remnants. One man was indifferent to the new truckload because he had found a box filled with chicken scraps. I recognized him as the same guy who had been going through rotten lettuce earlier. Christal confirmed my unpleasant theory moments later: the rancid chicken and lettuce, along with a few other finds, would make their way into a communal soup.

As I walked by myself to check in with the students, I was besieged by emotion. I was glad to be there as a witness but found myself on the verge of unraveling. I stopped for a moment to take in the enormity of this place, physically and symbolically. My students were fighting the sun, but concentrating more on helping their partners fill their colossal bags. A half dozen emaciated cows were grazing in the garbage, at which point I swore off all beef, Dominican or otherwise. Tractors were constantly rearranging the heaps of trash without regard for the workers or our group. It smelled of putrid meat. My thought at the beginning of the day had been of holding back tears, but now it shifted toward holding back my breakfast.

Keeping an eye on the students was difficult because I had to remain focused on where I was walking and what I was walking on. There had been a downpour the night before, so it was a muddy mess. I had devised one particular navigational strategy: seek out cardboard. This seemed to offer the most stability and didn't cause me to sink as walking on clothes did. In the back of my mind was a fearful image of me stepping on a flimsy box, my foot sliding deep under the muck, and my shoe being swallowed up as I lifted my leg. I didn't know how I would react to having to make my way on with only one shoe. Obstacles like a dog carcass and a hypodermic needle had already been reported, but luckily I didn't see either, and I hoped the students were just repeating rumors.

As I was skipping from a beer case to a radio box as though I were back in Boy Scouts, hopping from rock to rock across a calm river, the worst happened. I lost my footing, and a piece of cardboard slid out from underneath me to reveal a bright orange ooze. I immediately gagged and shut my mouth to hold things down. Somehow, I was able to minimize my outward reaction out of respect for those who worked there every day. I looked up; it seemed nobody had noticed. As I recovered from my awkward slide, I spotted a small shelter in the distance and wondered if people stayed here overnight. I was told that people used to do so at another dump on the island, but that it didn't happen anymore. That thought lingered until I noticed that a glob of orange gunk had attached itself to my shoe. For a moment it seemed to be spreading, so I closed my eyes and prayed that it was either the heat or my overactive imagination that made this blob appear alive and sinister. *Why did I have to use the word "blob," the movie that terrified me as a child?* With my eyes still closed, I tried to convince myself it was just a rotten mango that had gotten overexposed and started to bubble in the sun, but that didn't work, because the ooze soon had an astringent odor to go with it.

Searching for a distraction, I looked to my students, just as I do when times are tough back home. Right away, I saw that they were skipping around and jogging back under the blistering sun to help their partners. Those whose partners had filled a bag and who were ready for a break started kicking around a soccer ball and hacky sack. Two of our girls were chatting it up with six boys chewing on sugarcane who seemed very interested in them. One worker pulled out his cell phone—you can get used ones for less than ten dollars in the Dominican Republic—and was busy getting our students' first and last names so he could friend them on Facebook.

This anecdote shocks many people back home. "If they are only making around twenty-five dollars a month," they ask, "how can they afford a cell phone?" When I heard this question for the first time, before I could formulate an answer, I pictured a few of my eighth-grade students with tears in their eyes after a teacher confiscated their most prized possession. With a few, I have even noticed something akin to a "phantom limb" experience, where they reach for their phone only to realize it's gone. For the Dominican teens, I believe a cell phone opens many doors to make extra money. A disappointing example would be the frequency with which taxi drivers crowed about the women and drugs that could be mine for only a small finder's fee.

The last student I found was Marilyn. She had spent her entire time at the dump working with a pregnant woman, Miguelina. Marilyn spoke fluent Spanish, so I was happy she was getting a firsthand, unfiltered account of what life was like for those who must work in the dump. She told me later that Miguelina had lost much of her family, including her husband, in the 2010 Haitian earthquake. She lives at a nearby batey, and because she has no ID, "this is the only work that is available for her."

A few students had taken a break from gathering plastics and brought their partners to our bus for a water break. Our Molly Pitchers took our large water container off the bus and used the luggage compartment underneath as a shady place to fill up their bottles. As I stood there with another teacher, Ramona, I could tell her emotions had gotten the best of her. She told me that after a level of trust had been established, the twelve-year-old girl she was working with, who had started out as a vivacious worker, had suddenly said, "Please take me home with you. Those people you met aren't my real parents, and they beat me." Based on what Christal had said earlier, we deduced that this girl was a restavek, but we couldn't confirm anything else about her.

While trying to track down a woman who had worked in the dump for twenty-five years and delivered all eight of her children at home, I simultaneously eavesdropped on conversations and caught one of the workers playing matchmaker for our girls. "You would look good with my son," she said. Another man was explaining that he used to work in the rice fields but felt he was too far from his family, so he chose to work at the dump in spite of the lower pay and tougher conditions. My favorite moment was when two workers started arguing over us. One woman was complaining that her older friend had too many of our students helping her. "But they're my Americans!" was her reply, to which her coworker responded, "But you already have three!" The workers smiled as they argued and stopped as the older woman corralled her three helpers and headed in another direction.

People back home ask tons of questions about the dump, especially about the workers' demeanor. "You might not believe it, but they have this sort of 'whistle while you work' attitude toward the job," I say. They are definitely more joyful than serious. It is even common to hear a soulful tune as they rummage through that day's heap of trash, which is literally the previous night's garbage, as one teacher found out when her curiosity led her to open a small bag of recently used toilet paper. Christal confirmed this theory by saying, "They have fun with it but don't enjoy the work." The following are lyrics from a song we heard an older woman singing:

I'm singing; I cannot stop.
My dad fixed me like that.
Circumstances they unfit change;
It makes me anything,
Makes me so choose Christ.
My dad fixed me like that.
I'm singing in the sun, in the dark;
Anything that happens I'll be happy.
I have to sing; I cannot stop.
My dad fixed me like that.

When a few of our teachers pushed the dump workers to say how they felt about their job, one expressed disgust at a family member who was a sex worker. Christal translated that their sister was "shunned for working as a prostitute." As bad as the conditions at the dump are, the people there feel they work with dignity.

After an hour and a half, Kevin went around to let everyone know our time was almost up. We had been there for a relatively short while but taken in a lot. As I neared the bus, I was suddenly perplexed: I couldn't distinguish my students from the Haitian workers. Then I realized that the workers resembled my students because they were decked out in clothing that my students had been wearing just minutes before—hats, sneakers, shirts . . . and *pants*? I watched the good-byes, feeling both speechless and proud. The students were refusing to get on the bus, not because it was covered in grime, but because they could not stop talking with their partners or let go of their hands. There were a few tears, but mostly smiles. The day seemed to have empowered the students when it could easily have broken them. Many on the bus wore only underwear, including one adult (not me), and one teen appeared to have only a towel around his waist. On the drive home, Christal informed our students that since she had been bringing visitors to the dump, there had been a noticeable improvement in the workers' footwear over the years. I hoped the guys I had seen earlier in flip-flops and open-toed sandals would be the beneficiaries of today's collection of shoes.

One of our students gave a young worker a brand new Phillies hat before boarding the bus. In amazement, the boy kept putting it on and then taking it off to caress the material, to feel its fibers. His smile was immense, and his eyes were wide. I feared a taller boy might scoop it off his head, but he showed no signs of worry about losing what may have been one of his only material possessions.

The experience helped our students let go of material thoughts, too, and made it easier for them to feel that solidarity Kevin spoke of regularly. Eventually, with a lot of prodding, we got the last two students on the bus, and the doors slid closed. Many foreheads rested on the windows as we watched the workers return to their reality without a fuss or second thought. I turned around, and several of the students were rubbing each other's shoulders and offering comfort in other ways. The stench from the dump lingered, but more potent and lasting were the stories to be told.

George Santos, a native of Santo Domingo who has a friendly professorial look, was warned by his friends never to enter a batey while guiding a tour. He summed up his visit to the dump in these words:

> It is safe to say the trash dump is an awful place. But it is also a mirror, a final resting place for all the stuff we take for granted and interact with for short periods of time. This is where it all winds up.
>
> I tried remembering our goal for the group visit: to collect plastic bottles and help our temporary work partners gain some advantage over doing this work alone. I was a visitor helping this person out with his job: my garbage and yours. Yet I left with so much more than when I entered. I left behind part of my ignorance, and I took away a vaster knowledge of where my stuff winds up and how much what I discard is valued by those who lack access to any of it. I guess the cliché fits: my garbage is another man's treasure.
>
> I don't think of us as heroes. Well, Kevin obviously is. You kind of know this is how it works. But you don't know what it looks like, what it smells like, and how deeply it rocks your core to be, in a

small way, part of this whole system. You are so far removed from the process that you rarely second-guess it. Obviously, you disagree with it all, but you contribute your small part to make it real. I provide this garbage. I am part of a system that manages to pay so many so little. There is a feeling of ownership for this mess.

It also struck me that as much as others wanted to say these people are simply working here and any kind of work is dignifying, well, that's kind of easy to say from our vantage point. I didn't think there was much dignity left here. Truth be said, that lack of dignity was what got me. I was a wreck for hours after being there. The contrast was too strong, the reality too bare. Too much truth to keep my eyes dry.

Our shoes, as the tradition had become, stayed behind in the dump and got reassigned to someone who worked there. When I tried telling people in my neighborhood what I had witnessed, what we had done, how our shoes had stayed there, I was told, "You guys are being taken for fools if you think they will wear those shoes. They will probably go off somewhere and sell those."

Best-case scenario, these people are wrong, and the shoes are protecting the feet of the workers. Decent-case scenario, the workers will sell the shoes and make the equivalent of a few thousand plastic bottles collected without having to be in the dump. Help doesn't have to take the shape of the giver—just help. Stop convincing yourself that the best way to do something about it is by pretending it doesn't exist.

I was mad at the comment not because it came out of ignorance but because it so faithfully reflected mine. It took a day or two for my thinking to default back to normal. So I was mad at my own voice coming out of someone else's mouth. Mirrors are uncomfortable.

I had a fresh pair of shoes waiting for me back at the hotel, and more perspective dished out to me than I was ready to handle. Am I really part of all this? Welcome to the Matrix. Your eyes are now open. How do you like the red pill?

My thoughts also tiptoed around ideas of wages. Here in the dump, people's income is based on how many used plastic bottles they can gather. That is their livelihood. Their bags full of crushed and dirty bottles are tiny fractioned pieces of the Dominican Republic's minimum wage, which translates to about $180 a month—$45 a week, $9 a day, $1 an hour. If you make minimum wage in the DR, there is not much you have access to. Consuming locally is the only option, since locally grown foods, tubers, and vegetables are the cheapest.

When we made it to the dump, we saw some female vendors bringing *pan de agua* (a cheap local bakery bread) and fresh avocados. I asked them about their intent. They wanted to appeal to the trash collector workers. They would sell avocado sandwiches for about thirty-nine cents a sandwich. I discreetly reached into my pocket and paid for every avocado they carried and also their bread. I told them not to give the food away over there, as it may have caused a feeding frenzy. I just asked them to lower the prices even more that day. I don't know what they did. Did they take me for a ride? Either way, my gesture may have helped anywhere from two to thirty people, depending on what the vendors did—all for the sum of eleven dollars. Wealth is so relative. Understanding poverty without living it is comparable to trying to understand never owning shoes while wearing comfy loafers.

The living wage in the Dominican Republic, the *canasta familiar*, is actually three times the minimum wage. When you are making a living wage, you can afford to feed a small family for a month with locally grown food, no imports of any kind, with very little leeway. Most people making minimum wage are two-thirds away from that standard of living. Multiply the living wage by two, by three, or by four, and you can live comfortably. Divide the living wage by any number, and you experience poverty. The math is simple. The reality is complex.

This is one of the reasons that the haves need to give handouts and tips to the have-nots so often. It is one of the unspoken ways Dominican society tries to make up for the unbearable load on the bottom end of the financial spectrum. If race is a problem in the DR, class is an even deeper and more profound issue. Being middle class or upper middle class means you have to constantly be tipping, helping, aiding, and even lending at times, with little chance of the money coming back. It also means any hired help you have cannot take care of basic needs like medical care or dental care, so those handouts are also expected. It does make for some interesting budgeting. The other choice is to simply turn away and pretend it is not your problem. Pick your evil.

I mention the middle and upper middle classes because the high class of the Dominican Republic is a bit of a different beast. To this class, living wage and minimum wage are hypothetical concepts. Having inherited patterns of master-servant relationships from generations of wealth, their contact with poverty is rare. It usually happens through charities, institutions, or programs of some kind. While out and about, their hired help takes care of tipping workers, street beggars, maids, nannies, gardeners, and others. There is very little contact with needy people for several reasons, foremost being personal security.

A year after the student trip in 2010, we had a get-together where many of us shared our thoughts about the tour. The dump—the event with the least expectations but the greatest impact—was the most talked-about experience. When asked her thoughts on the trip as a whole, Marilyn, a college student, said, "As a teen, you don't think you can make a difference. Kevin planted this seed for us. You have to absorb it all. It's our second nature to want to change things. I've learned that often it's better to just absorb what's in front of you. It takes immersing yourself in a difficult environment to really learn." The dump, she continued, "was very real. It changed the way I see things. It changed the way I watch television and read. I process things so much differently now. I understand things a lot better, especially the politics of it."

Marilyn also spoke directly about her time with Miguelina. "She approached me. Fortunately, she spoke Spanish. Immediately, she trusted me. She was twenty and pregnant with twins and lived in a batey with her son. She emigrated from Haiti. During the earthquake she lost her parents," she said. "You don't think twice about where the garbage is going. Many see Haitians as good enough to do labor that's at the bottom. I don't think I was prepared for something of that magnitude. Including traveling, her workday is something like from five in the morning to four in the afternoon. I know there are a lot of Miguelinas in the world."

Our superintendent, Dr. Rocco Tomazic, who was on the trip, shared his thoughts about Kevin: "It's easy to preach. He never does that. He stood back; he made sure we were focused but didn't crowd into the space." Of his dump partner, he said, "I noticed how excited she was when we found a clean plastic bottle. What you really learn is about that person, how she's living, how she sees you. You walk away different than just appreciating and valuing what you have. Who could smile working every day in a garbage dump? We enjoyed it because we were learning, not because we were doing something good."

During the teacher tour, George Santos, who teaches at a private school where teachers earn four to seven times more than their public school counterparts, revealed a bit of information that left all of us speechless: he has two maids. When we interrupted his train of thought to ask him to go back to the part about his housekeepers, he seemed genuinely confused about our inquiries. I knew I would have to get something from him in writing on the topic, or others would have as difficult a time understanding his response as we did. The following is George's take on hired help:

> Did you read the book or watch the movie *The Help*? There are descriptions there that definitely match the reality of the Dominican Republic when it comes to domestic workers. Maids are very common in the DR, so much so that some maids have maids. They are usually in charge of laundry, cooking, cleaning the entire house, making beds, mopping floors, cleaning incidentals, and running the kitchen.
>
> The average maid in the Dominican Republic makes about $250 a month. To date, they have no health insurance system, no Social Security system, and absolutely no pension plan or retirement funds set aside for them. Only with their salary must they pay for the basics and the not-so-basics of everyday life, with little if any money going into their savings.
>
> It is important to remember, however, that public school teachers also make about $250 a month. So wages in the Dominican Republic are not really high for any profession, much less people who are part of the working class.
>
> A maid may work in a private home of a Dominican family anywhere between one and forty years. In the past, maids would spend the night regularly where they worked. Nowadays, it has

shifted more to working from seven in the morning until about six in the evening.

Maids do not seem to have a lot of rights as workers, but there are basic laws covering every single person employed, whether formally or informally. If you were to fire a maid and withhold her salary for no apparent reason, or withhold her Christmas bonus, which by law belongs to her, a maid could go to the government's Department of Labor Rights and file a claim. The employer is almost always forced to pay that maid's salary or benefits.

In the Dominican Republic, there are very generous and wonderful employers who help maids move forward, get a better education, pay for things they could not afford, and improve their overall lives. There are maids who stay with a family for many years and help raise that family so closely they become part of it. Many nannies and maids grow so close to family members, they even become informal advisers and motherly or grandmotherly figures.

There are also many employers who hire maids and take to treating them very poorly. There are people who demand more than is reasonable from their maids and refuse to help them if they have a problem they can't resolve or can't afford, like a medical issue. Forcing them to work longer hours than they reasonably can is common. Some people even threaten to fire maids when they ask for basic things.

The culture of how to treat a maid is not written in stone. It varies from person to person. The truth is that they are as integral a part of Dominican society as the rest of its members. There are, however, some unwritten rules followed very consistently from home to home when it comes to maids. One of them is that maids do not sit and eat at the table with the rest of the family; they eat in a separate space or at a separate table or in a back room. They would find it uncomfortable to be invited to sit at the table and eat with the rest of the family, because it is such a nonpractice.

Many families require maids to wear a uniform, a sort of outfit with big buttons in the front that looks very much like a nanny uniform. This has never been a practice with maids I've had in my own home, so I don't really understand what purpose it serves. Of course, there is the obvious benefit of having a uniform: keeping your regular clothes from everyday wear and tear. I can see that part of it being a benefit, especially since the employer buys the uniform.

Once, I mustered the courage to ask some people why they buy uniforms for their maids. The answer I got was a bit of a shocker: "I like them to have uniforms because uniforms make them look plain and simple. I don't want to have my maids walking around the house in tight jeans or tight shirts or skirts showing their bodies off to my husband, who could fall into temptation." This answer led me to conclude that uniforms definitely serve more than the obvious purposes. I thought about how this society (and a few other, similar ones) approaches men and our ability to act responsibly for ourselves. I found it fascinating to hear that instead of talking to your own husband about the importance of fidelity in your relationship, you would simply manage the environment around him in a way that prevents your husband from being unfaithful.

It's interesting to observe that society seems to excuse men here in the Dominican Republic from being accountable for their own actions, to the point that they are not asked directly to act responsibly. So put a clown uniform on your maid to keep your husband faithful.

Sometimes the subtlest pieces of information seem to speak volumes about the truth of a society. That doesn't mean it is good or bad; it is what it is. When it comes to maids, however, we do need to understand that they are all part of an economic system. These jobs exist because the society demands it, and the job provides a limited working class with choices that, without these jobs, would continue to be even more limited.

I'm not saying being a maid is the best profession for everybody, but I am saying it is one form of existence. They need more rights and more benefits, and they have a definite place in Dominican society. I don't see it changing anytime soon, because the convenience of maids far outweighs their costs. The average Dominican family usually sets aside a small part of its budget for a maid's salary at some level. Self-sufficiency is not high on our priority list.

Interestingly enough, maids here also have their own class system. There are maids in the lowest ranks who are assistants to other maids or apprentices, or who might just be getting started and are really young. Many times, these maids don't even make a salary because they don't know enough yet and are just learning the ropes.

A maid's place in society is equivalent to the place in society of the family she works for. A maid working for an average middle-class family in the Dominican Republic will have basic responsibilities in that home. A maid working in a low-income family might have a closer relationship to the family because of their proximity socially. Her wages might be lower but her schedule much more flexible.

On the other end of the spectrum, you have maids who work for the wealthiest of Dominicans. These maids actually have ranks. Some of them are head maids in charge of maids under them, and some earn very significant salaries and have valuable places both in their families and in society. They are often well traveled, well read, very educated, and enjoy benefits that perhaps even white-collar workers in the Dominican Republic do not have access to.

The topic of maids is not a simple one to explain or understand. Yet, looking at Dominican society up close, there is little evidence of a change at that level being near or even necessary. But it is overdue to implement some systems for health care and social security that reach this working class that is so intricate a part of Dominican society.

A team-building activity

Chapter 7
A NEVER-ENDING SOMETHING SPECIAL

Abre las hojas del viento, mi vida, ponle una montura al río, cabalga, y si te da frío, te arropas con la piel de las estrellas. (Open the leaves of the wind, my love, put a horse seat on the river, ride it, and if you get cold, put a blanket of stars on to warm you.) *Amapola* by Juan Luis Guerra

The ninety-minute ride north from the "heart city" of Santiago to Los Brazos, where we would be staying at El Jardín de los Niños (The Children's Garden) for a couple of days, required us to navigate one of the three crooked backbones of the Dominican Republic. For those who find a scenic drive through the countryside soothing, I couldn't recommend anything more tranquil than a trip through the

Septentrional mountain range. It's where you most feel the floral flavors and tropical tones of the Dominican Republic unfold.

As we approached the verdant mountains, covered in a lush carpet of vegetation, we were greeted by a dozen young men lounging on their motorcycles, legs dangling over the handlebars, stealing some shade. When our teenage girls smiled back, the men threw them handfuls of kisses. At that point I feared our students had "engaged."

Fortunately, we were in a covered automobile, so the only response from our girls was mildly suppressed giggles that didn't encourage the men to take up a chase. On other trips, when we rode in the back of pickup trucks, the scent of our teens spread like catnip through the streets, and the men were quick to jump on their bikes, getting within a foot of our rickety ride and showering the young ladies with an assortment of flowers, *empanadas*, and phone numbers.

At the foothills of the mountains were noticeable differences from what we had seen so far in Santo Domingo and Santiago. The dogs were much better fed and walked with their heads pointing amicably upward. Dominican children waved and screamed toward our bus, "Hi, Americans!" while elbowing one another in fits of laughter. Laundry baked in the sun, hanging on the waist-high, rusty wire fencing separating spacious home plots. The cows even seemed more relaxed as they grazed in the open along a rushing, muddy river.

Hugging the narrow mountain roads were a mix of mangled guardrails streaked with paint by errant drivers; high, jagged rock walls; and vendor stands selling produce dirt-cheap. Against a foggy backdrop, small trees sprouted along barbed-wire fences in place of sidewalks. Along the sides of the street were the dark, dirty *zanjas* (irrigation canals), which snatch the occasional motorcycle with rider still attached into their depths. There was also a dichotomy between the few multistory homes with satellites and the abundance of abandoned ones falling to pieces.

Just minutes into our climb, Yunior recommended we open the windows. I was the first to slide mine open, because I figured he wanted us to savor the morning air and whatever Caribbean aromas it carried. Before I could distinguish any particular scents, though, as I would if tasting a fine wine, I noticed that the country sounds had come alive—kids playing, motorcycles puttering, and tropical birds squawking. This sudden clarity was because the air conditioner had gone silent. Several startled looks were thrown Yunior's way, and he explained that the climb was so strenuous on the bus that the driver had to kill the air-conditioner to allow more energy to go toward the engine. If it hadn't been early in the morning and a path of shade hadn't covered the road, Yunior might have had a mutiny on his hands.

So we battled uphill, engine sputtering and gears grinding, at about five miles per hour, which at least offered us longer, clearer glimpses of our surroundings. I especially enjoyed noting the particulars of each *colmado*. They were painted vibrant blues and yellows, with bundles of bananas or fatty ribs suspended from each store window. The interior walls were lined with an artfully stacked array of canned and bottled goods, reminiscent of an Andy Warhol painting.

A pregnant woman leaned against a door with a welcoming smile while her child played nearby. Homes lined the winding streets, and the children played along narrowly worn paths that were dangerously close to the road. A light toot on the horn from most oncoming traffic was a reminder to the kids to be vigilant. Despite the dusty air and choking automobile fumes, the stores were immaculately clean.

The homes were painted in bright pastels. ("The brighter the better" is a popular phrase when discussing local architecture.) While the façades had been methodically constructed to create smooth but sturdy surfaces, the backs of the homes often revealed cinderblock skeletons.[36] This realization got me thinking about how the Dominican Republic appears paradisiacal on the surface, but when you crane your neck to check out things around back, you notice its many vulnerabilities.

When we reached the peak and saw Santiago anew, the country unfolded in undulating greens, revealing antiquated, agriculturally inspired terraces. The air-conditioning kicked back on, and we were suddenly slaloming down the curvy mountain roads, our driver making up for lost time. The red, white, and blue Brugal rum signs announcing the next towns were a blur, as were the faces adorning a plethora of faded political posters.

This bucolic landscape easily lifted my mind and body to another dimension. The streams of pink and purple flowers decorating each turn hypnotized me. The decades-old, delicately constructed stone walls

---

[36] Home conditions in the DR are often reflective of whether the residents have family in the United States.

The Dominican Experiment

were tempting invitations to stay behind. The abandoned brick homes with thatched roofs piqued my curiosity. The men in jeans and button-down shirts slashing at the overgrowth with machetes made me crave a simpler way of life. I felt uninhibited, welcoming the next sensation, allowing everything in. Then, suddenly—I fell back into reality. Spray-painted in the distance was sloppy handwriting: *"Fuera los Haitianos!"* The jagged letters were written in a way that left me expecting a painful explanation.

Yunior translated the message: "Haitians, go home!"

The students and I cringed as we tried to process this obscenity and put it into context. But before I could start a discussion about it, Kevin grabbed the microphone to give his introduction to our next stop. He told the students that we were changing things up a bit and would be camping for the next few days on grounds owned by a Canadian woman named Paulina who takes in orphans and children whose families cannot afford to support them. He said that Paulina was like a mother bear, very protective of her cubs, and that she ran a tight ship. That said, we would be expected to clean up after ourselves, use appropriate language, and not rile up the hippopotamus-size pig named Gordo.

As we settled into the grounds at Jardín, reminiscent of a pastoral sleepaway camp where children have a wealth of adventures to choose from, our group made the mental transition from three-star accommodations with air-conditioning to roughing it. But before the students could become grumpy, Paulina's group of about a dozen teens and more little ones popped up to help with our luggage, and the mingling began. Our plan had been to do a few group activities, but Kevin's gut told him we should take a softer approach with this unique bunch. Here and there, our students and theirs took a moment to see where everyone was linguistically and then did what teens do best: talk about everything. The light conversations were followed by card games, hair braiding, and jump rope, just as if they were back on some school yard, enjoying the carefree days of their youth. It was nice to see kids just being kids.

After two days with the Jardín teens, exploring the surroundings and staying up late each night around the fire, we wanted to have a closing activity together. Instead of organizing something formal, we decided that a nice day at the beach in Cabarete, famous for windsurfing because of its strong, constant breeze, would be just the thing. Since transportation on the island is expensive, and Paulina's teens' swimming experience was limited to a rushing river downhill from their acreage, Kevin doubted they had had many opportunities to go to the beach. (Most of our students accompanied their counterparts to that river to give river-bathing a go. I suppressed the urge to go along so I could see their reactions to leaping out of their comfort zones with this one. Instead, I watched them walk off in their swimsuits, arms locked with one another and a bucket with soap and shampoo dangling at their side.)

For most of our time at *la playa*, half of the teens hung back by the beach chairs while the rest played in the water, throwing a football back and forth, boys versus girls. I believe the Jardín teens who stayed by the chairs did so because they appreciated the chance to interact with the American parents, since they don't have many chats with adults other than Paulina.

In addition to getting to know the Jardín crew better, the parents also stepped up by making sure their teens had some good laughs. When Liz, a forty-something-year-old Jewish mother with a doctorate, hiked up her pants, put on one teen's hat sideways, and started to bob back and forth to a beat she found somewhere inside her, the eyes of the Jardín teens became even brighter, and they ran to grab the others who weren't nearby so they didn't miss the unbelievable rap show. I have always felt that being able to make fun of yourself to put a smile on a child's face is one of the noblest character traits. Releasing the need for control and allowing yourself to be laughed at is a beautiful gift that leaves a lasting impression. That's probably why karaoke is so popular.

While we were on the beach, another mother noticed that only the American teens were buying snacks and drinks from the nearby vendors and restaurants. With this realization, she got up and tested the waters by buying a large fruit punch and offering it to the Jardín kids. One by one they declined, as she had half expected. As she was running out of teens to offer the drink to, she did what any good mother would do—she refused to take no for an answer. So when she got near the end of the group, she stopped asking and forced the cup on an unsuspecting teen. (It's tough for people to accept charity, but when you take the choice out of the equation, it allows people to save face and not think twice about the gesture.) As she was heading back to her chair, the mom seemed to wonder if she had been too assertive. But as she glanced back, she noticed an amazing moment developing. Not only was the boy enjoying the drink, and not only was he sharing it with those who had declined the initial offer, but he was also making sure each member of his family got at least one ice cube from the cup.

To say the Jardín teens are a family is an understatement. They are all responsible for a litany of chores, from cooking and cleaning to chopping wood and building the day's fire. They are as tight-knit of a family as you can get. Paulina has really created something special there. And—unlike the HIV/AIDS orphanage we visited in past years, which requires children to leave when they turn sixteen, whether or not a secure home has been found for them—Paulina has promised all her children that when they decide to become independent, start a career, or get married, a house on her large plot of land awaits them. This is a crucial part of Jardín: knowing that life in this fairy-tale setting, tucked away from the harsh realities of the island (not without hard work and discipline, of course), doesn't have to end. And isn't that what we all want—a never-ending something special?

La playa

Chapter 8
DID THEY JUST THROW SOMETHING AT US?

*Si el destino te lanza un cuchillo, hay dos formas
de atraparlo: por el filo o por el mango.*
(If fate throws a knife at you, there are two ways of
catching it: by the blade or by the handle.)

The sights and sounds of a Dominican beach are mesmerizing: an oasis of turquoise water lapping onto soft beige sand, complete with Spanish rhythms and Creole whispers. Many of the one-room shack restaurants hugging the typical beach are staffed by young women who wag their index fingers along with bachata songs, often teary-eyed.

While taking in the Caribbean ambience under a palm tree, sitting comfortably on plastic furniture held steady by the ubiquitous green

Presidente umbrella and perusing a colorful menu in four languages (English, French, German, and Spanish), which I was glad to see didn't have pizza with Viagra as a topping as did the previous day's restaurant, I engaged in light conversation with a waitress with two birthdays (the day she was actually born and the birth date on all her identification—months later when her father was able to get her listed into the books) who was scratching a vaccination scar on her left shoulder. "*¿Por qué tan triste?*" (Why are you so sad?) I asked after declining her offer of *mamajuana* (rum, red wine, honey, oak, and other herbs) and instead opting for a foamy blend of German malt and condensed milk, a drink believed to imbue strength. She waved her hand as if it were nothing, took a big bite of a *tostón* (fried plantain slice), and blamed the music, but her distant gaze hinted at a promiscuous lover. I offered to buy her a drink, and when she popped off the top, the lid also came off her drama. In a nutshell, she had two mouths to feed and not even a good-bye from her man. I asked her about child support and got a blank stare. Her English was much better than my Spanish, and once she grasped the concept, she just shook her head.

While Kevin packed in more attractions than seemed physically possible to experience in one week, touring the southern and northern coasts with lively waterfalls in between, he still managed to offer the teens an entire day at the beach. They thought he was being benevolent, but it was really a way of giving them yet another window into Dominican culture.

When we arrived, after passing a row of pastel street shops selling items from rusty machetes to artisan jewelry, with very hands-on vendors literally pulling our students into their stores, it was still early in the morning, and the beach was cluttered with the previous day's trash. Most of the vendors were raking their storefront areas to give themselves the most welcoming appearance. At one store, a six-year-old, missing her two front teeth[37] and wearing pink flower barrettes, was

---

[37] In the DR, when a child's tooth falls out, she is told to throw it as far as she could so that *Ratoncito* (Little Mouse) *Miguel* can find it and get her a replacement.

using a miniature rake and imitating her father as he collected a pile of bruised fruit, large leaves, and plastic bags.

Walking with the students had me on full alert in some ways but relaxed in others. A guide from our teacher tours informed me that he is always armed when leading teenagers from city to city. I was obviously not packing heat, but it was as if my head was on a swivel as we escorted them to a nice spot. I have heard that locals enjoy messing with young, boisterous Americans, but in my many visits, I have never seen anyone cross the line.[38] But while harassment is one hurdle we've managed to avoid on our trips, I still walk close to the students, because I can never forget the trusting eyes of their parents back at the airport as they waved good-bye. Plus, it's when you let your guard down that bad things seem to happen. Fortunately, our beach experience was smooth sailing, followed by actual smooth sailing out in the cove as the students went snorkeling above the coral reefs with the brightest, bluest fish.

My first experience on a Dominican beach, not as part of a tour group, was quite memorable. A college friend and I were walking the worn path along the shops, and not a minute went by that we didn't have to give a *"No, gracias"* or an apologetic wave to an offer of renting beach chairs for the day. (In the relaxed atmosphere of the beach, I can get away with rejecting vendors' offers. On the streets, though, I strictly follow Kevin's golden rule and avoid any form of engagement, refusing to answer their proposals even with a rejection. Keeping in mind that facial gestures are a popular form of communication in the Dominican Republic, I guard constantly against glances or expressions that could be misconstrued. Many Dominicans have a difficult time grasping Americans' need for personal space, because they are on the other side of the spectrum, where there is always room to fit another person in a bus or at a table. It feels rude to flat-out ignore vendors and others on the streets, but in this case, nice guys definitely finish last, often finding themselves dragged into stores and the doors locked behind them.)

The farther my college buddy and I walked down the beach, the more generous the offers got. One guy with a big smile and a bigger

---

[38] A former student recently attended a study abroad orientation, and she couldn't wait to tell me that the first bit of advice they received was not to reinforce the stereotype that Americans are "loud and obnoxious."

belly said he had a special deal for the two of us: a free drink with a rental chair. We smiled appreciatively but passed. The day after, during our ritual walk to the vendor with the Charlie Chaplin moustache, we made eye contact with the big-bellied vendor, and he obviously remembered us—proprietors have impeccable memories—so he upped the ante and offered a free lunch: *el plato del día* (the dish of the day). We looked at each other, impressed by the bargain, but politely told him that we already had a spot. On the third day, as we neared the guy of generous offers, my friend suggested we entertain the next offer because he sensed the vendor would go even higher. My gut told me this would be a mistake, but I allowed him to stray from our ground rules because he needed to learn the lesson for himself.

"Rent two beach chairs, and you can sleep with my wife," the vendor declared. Before I could check my friend's expression, the vendor gestured toward an attractive female significantly younger than he, and she smiled *directly at us*. I immediately turned to my friend and gave him a firm "I told you so!" look—not that I had expected to hear anything that shocking. Our stunned faces must have alerted the vendor that we had been thinking more along the lines of a free seafood lunch.

As we arrived at our regular guy's shop in a stupor, we took our normal place and ordered *sancocho* (the national dish of the Dominican Republic, a soup with chunks of meat and vegetables, served with the caution, "Be prepared to sweat"). My friend and I glanced at each other several times over the next few minutes before either of us was able to put words to our feelings. Moments later, the vendor's wife came sauntering toward us in a soft white bikini and a light, porous skirt, as if to confirm that the offer was still on the table. Our faces, of course, left no doubt that we were unaccustomed to this type of bartering and didn't know where to begin in terms of respectfully declining. She must have sensed our discomfort, and she vanished, along with our confidence that we were starting to get the hang of the Dominican lifestyle.

As I was trying to wrap my mind around what had just transpired, I spotted next to us a sixty-year-old white man with a twenty-year-old Dominican woman, a common sight on the island. She was wearing a larimar[39] ring and designer sunglasses. While I am often told that age doesn't matter when it comes to relationships in the Dominican

---

[39] Larimar is a sometimes sky blue, sometimes turquoise stone native only to the DR.

Republic, others suggest that young women seek out much older men because they have developed a distaste for the machismo attitude of Dominican guys their age, or because they are focusing on their family and future.

These two episodes left me reflecting on people's hierarchy of needs. When you aren't able to secure basic necessities such as shelter and food, your wants are quickly trumped. I don't tell these stories to be judgmental, but because cultural differences fascinate me. Why are some things, like dating, entirely different just a short plane ride away? And how did they evolve that way? I think the strongest parts of my character have developed as a result of my travel experiences and my constant examining and reexamining of a culture other than the one in which I grew up. Contemplating these idiosyncrasies has been beneficial in that I have become more dedicated to learning a second language, more likely to linger at a restaurant long after the bill has arrived, and significantly less desirous of personal space.

If you are observant, you learn with time that different is not synonymous with worse. You learn to think outside the proverbial box. Letting go of judgments and assumptions that where you come from is better leads to the healthiest perspective on life one can obtain.

If Dominican vendors seem like a determined lot, there's another segment of Dominican society that is even more unrelenting. They aren't as overtly assertive as the peddlers of goods, but what they lack in aggressiveness they make up for in persistence.

When Kevin and I picked out chairs for a day of decompressing between the student and teacher tours, we chose a shaded area, my preference. Local families started arriving at the same time. There were two catamarans in the distance, divers cavorting over a labyrinth of coral reefs, and two young Dominican brothers in a kayak. We discovered some prime real estate, and Kevin quickly went off to the water. Once he left, the corgi made her move.

I often wonder if it is the food or the companionship the *perros* are more interested in obtaining. It started off with a variation of the kids' game "red light, green light." As soon as we made eye contact, she stopped, and when I turned away, she approached—a strategy she may have picked up from the beach vendors. Eventually, she realized it was safe to come all the way. She approached with her head lowered, not begging. I fought the urge to pet her, because she was a bit mangy and regularly gnawing at her backside.

I felt bad because I didn't have any food just yet, and seeing as we were by the ocean, I wondered how much access this *viralata* (underdog or "tin flipper") had to fresh water. I picked up my water bottle, and she immediately perked up. She was quite adept at giving appropriate feedback. I offered her a little drink by pouring the bottle, and she took a few licks but seemed disappointed with my mechanics. I had nothing in my bag, and knowing how many locals feel about strays, I doubted my request for a bowl would go over well. That's when I spotted something the dog appeared to be looking at: Kevin's rubber sandal. I looked at the dog, and I swear she nodded. I checked on Kevin, who was drifting along the waves, and gave it a go. I grabbed his sandal, pointed the heel toward the dog and began to pour. The water hit the toe and trickled into a pool at the heel, which served as a basin. She immediately started lapping it up. Each time I added water, her tail wagged more enthusiastically. When my bottle ran out, the dog went back to the foot of my chair, and I made sure to place Kevin's wet sandal directly in the sun.

Back in her shady spot under my feet, the dog looked off into the distance. After a couple of minutes she finally let her guard down, closed her eyes, and drifted off. The next moment, the owner of the chairs came huffing by and yelled her awake, and she darted off, barely avoiding the impact of his foot. The abuse of dogs by these frustrated men is an obvious form of displaced anger.

After casting a few looks in my direction from a safe distance, the dog began to burrow in the hot sand. She attacked the beach with her nose and feet, and when she reached cooler ground she stretched out on her side. All I could do was offer an apologetic look for the human race.

Kevin returned after five minutes and toweled off. He looked down at his sandals, and I nonchalantly turned the other way. He saw immediately that one was damp and the other wasn't, but the heat won out, and the thought seemed to evaporate from his mind.

He sat down, and we ordered food, for which the vendor later tried to overcharge me. I make it a habit to examine *la cuenta* thoroughly each time I eat, and right away I noticed a mistake: 300 and 30 do not add up to 430. I pointed out the error, and he ignored me. I became firmer. After four detailed explanations, the man still wouldn't budge and demanded his money. That was when I called in my muscle. I grabbed Kevin and handed him the bill. "Does this look right to you?" He noticed the obvious blunder and just stared at the guy with his give-me-a-break look. Kevin's Spanish is much better than mine, as is his resolve not to be taken advantage of. It only took him one try to get the guy to relent. The vendor feigned apologetic, patted my shoulder, and rewrote the bill. As we were leaving, I gave him a small smirk because Kevin had mentioned that later in the week he would be bringing a group of teachers to rent chairs, and I wanted the guy to realize that his attempt to be slick had cost him a host of future sales.

The other half of the beach where we stayed is more upbeat and animated. It's typically a family affair, especially on weekends. Thriftiness prevails: the men haul overstuffed coolers, and the women carry five-gallon stove pots of spaghetti that last them well after the sun goes down. An elderly, white chair vendor complained, "Dominicans want to pay half price for a chair and fit four people on it." His rant fell on deaf ears, but he forced me to listen to the same thing every day.

I never really enjoyed alcohol in the extreme heat, but there's no shortage of it on the beach; it's the nation's number two moneymaker after tourism. When finished, the locals bury the dead soldiers upside down in a row that serves as a monument to their inebriation. Many bring their beers into the water, and the occasional glass shard you step on is an annoying reminder.

Once you're comfortably seated on a beach chair, a steady barrage of walking vendors materialize at your feet, offering all types of services: hair-braiding, massages, necklaces, guitar solos, and edibles such as shrimp, oysters, and—my favorite—*dulces de coco* (coconut sweets). Coconuts are said to be nature's laxative, which fulfilled none of our needs because during our time on the island, all bathroom issues were in the opposite realm.

There is about an even split between Dominican and Haitian vendors, all of whom wear blue button-down shirts and a vendor's license tag to prove they are part of the local federation. The Haitian women typically carry an assortment of luscious fruit in a tub that rests on their heads, kept secure by a small towel and uncanny balance. A friend, and newbie to the island, once joked in amazement at the amount and diversity of items the women can corral in one tub, "It's like they've got the entire *colmado* in there!"

During my downtime between the student and teacher tours, I prefer a smaller, more secluded beach. I don't think it even has a name; they just call it *la playa*. Here, a constant breeze quickly carries you away to another world. The water is calm, and you have to walk out a quarter mile before it reaches your knees. Every day around noon, the young fishermen cross the shore with crawfish dangling from a rusty hook, dragging it in the water to keep the crustaceans, and thus their investment, alive. Harpoons rest on their shoulders and diving gear hangs from the back of their rucksacks. An older man with a bundled seine follows closely behind.

In contrast to these travel-guide scenes, soldiers in full fatigues with automatic rifles regularly patrol the beach. They're eerily similar to those who guard the ATMs. Perhaps both have the same job: protecting their investments.

While this smaller beach is calmer, it can be more dangerous to the unsuspecting *gringo*. The first thing I do when considering a lounge chair at this beach is to take inventory overhead. While it's rare to see a coconut fall, because the locals have a sixth sense for when they are ripe and ready to chop down, the unpredictable almond and palm trees drop surprises with enough frequency to interrupt any significant napping. It took getting hit three times in a one-hour span for me to realize that not seeing any almonds directly overhead was not good enough reconnaissance, because there are layers to the porous canopy, and the winds are strong enough to carry these hazards quite a distance. Even after I requested an umbrella, nature's bombs still found a way to wreak havoc on my *siesta*.

I've often heard that falling objects from trees injure and even kill more tourists each year in the Dominican Republic than mosquito-based diseases or street scuffles. During the student tour, when our group was chatting with a Peace Corps worker, there was a rustling of leaves and a sudden thud near the adults. We were all shaken by the noise, and one parent blurted out, "Did they just throw something at us?"

Diana Braisted, Dedé Mirabal, and Asha Martin

Chapter 9
But I *Am* Black!

El ladrón juzga por su propia condición.
(The thief judges from his own condition.)

To explore the Dominican Republic—from *la capital* in the south to the Amber Coast in the north, and places in between like Jarabacoa (the "city of everlasting spring"), with its abundant fields of strawberries and supposedly the only apple trees on the island—one must be prepared for some literal and figurative bumps in the road. Our bus rides served as nice bits of downtime when we could process the recent transformative experiences and start formulating questions from the culture shock. If you are in the thirty-and-older crowd, as I am, a two-hour bus ride is also a perfect opportunity to indulge in a nice nap, as your eyes grow heavy from gazing at mountaintops. But don't get too mesmerized by the scenery, regardless of where you are, or you might do something like rub your leg along a hot motorcycle tailpipe, which initially felt like a snake had jumped out and bit me. As soon as it happened, a local was quick to offer a remedy of lime and salt, which left me puzzled and his buddies laughing, not so much at me as at an inside joke.

Kevin used our time on the bus practically. During the first ten minutes of each ride, he made a smooth transition from what we had seen the previous day to what we were about to experience. There was an underlying thread connecting all of our excursions, and for the themes that weren't so obvious, it was enjoyable to listen to Kevin as he guided the students to connect the dots. After a brief tie-in of the major tour themes (injustice, poverty, structural racism, etc.) in Kevin's smooth voice—and a reminder, "What you are learning about here takes place in most countries"—everyone would be nodding in understanding (and a few continued the motion, bobbing toward a sound sleep).

About five minutes before we arrived at the day's destination, Kevin would grab the microphone again, share a joke, and then provide a delicate transition from relaxing respite to exciting encounter. Having our own personal experts on the issues before us, like Kevin and Yunior, was the most valuable aspect of the trip. Some of my friends prefer to jump into things cold, but I always appreciate an artwork more after someone has enlightened me on what's behind the brushstrokes.

The major museum in Santiago is the Centro León. It has a proud beige and cream façade, an array of welcoming palm trees, a wide walkway over a fountain pool that you must cross to enter, and an inscribed message overhead for visitors: *El museo es una escuela, el artista aprende a comunicarse, el público aprende a hacer conexiones* (The museum is a school, the artist learns to communicate, the audience learns to make connections). Upon walking into the lobby, before you even pay your entrance fee, you catch a glimpse of the first artwork on display: *El descubrimiento del 70* (by Colectivo Shampoo in 2003), a life-size motorcycle immersed in amber as if it were an ancient, preserved specimen. I have visited the museum several times, and each time that piece conjures different feelings.

In the first exhibit, *Signos de identidad* (*Signs of Identity*), where television screens above us showed colorful faces, young and old, our guide asked us which ones we thought were Caribbean. As she nodded at the students' answers, I quickly picked up on her point: People of the Caribbean come in every shape, size, and color.

After she had walked us through the first few sections, we came to my favorite exhibit: a comparison of African and Spanish cultural relics. Off to the right, behind glass, were the Spanish artifacts, perched on pedestals and nestled on silk in fancy wooden boxes. On the other side, partly blocked by a large, wooden sugarcane extractor, are the African items. Many visitors miss these entirely because the display is concealed behind dull two-by-fours with eyeholes too narrow to fit your hand through, as if the display were under construction. The Spanish art is an illuminated collection of stone wheels, ancient currency, fancy kitchenware and dinnerware, jewelry, tools, and antique dominos and dice—pieces that embody progress and ingenuity. Behind the drab wall are African drums and horns (similar to the ones we saw at the Vodou ceremony), primitive artworks, masks, and wooden hair picks—items that imply simplicity.

The message couldn't be more obvious: in the Dominican Republic, the people's Spanish roots are highlighted and their African heritage is intentionally obscured. Our museum tour guide did tell us, "What is African in our heritage is vibrant and colorful, and still alive and present in the everyday lives of Dominicans." But what is of Spanish descent is displayed in an exaggerated way, even though much of it is old and rusty—relics of a past that does not resonate much in contemporary Dominican culture. "We are a result of the African and Spanish mixture," the guide said. This display and the guide's comments leave me hopeful each time, and I cherish the moment when the students are presented with this dichotomy.

The Dominicans I have built the closest relationships with over the years have all made the same comment—"all Dominicans have African in their blood"—but they only say this when we are talking one-on-one. When expressed publicly, this idea leads to either a major identity transformation or plain rejection. Jenny, a woman with strong Spanish features, whom we met through a humanitarian group we work with, was in disbelief when she first heard this concept in her twenties. "I spent two days in front of a mirror, trying to see which part of my body was black," she said.

Jenny then spoke about the month and a half of frustration in which she lightened her hair, researched her ancestry, and hounded her mother for answers. "In the end," she said, "I lost a lot of friends because I embraced my black roots. But I *am* black!" She said she walked away from the experience with her head held higher and gained "new friends, new life, and a new perspective."

Occasionally, after I present this theory in class, I have Dominican students return the next day with angry responses and flat-out denials from their parents.

Here are George Santos's thoughts on the exhibit:

> A lot can be said as to what the origins of this racial denial might be. Centro León may well be one of the few institutions that have ever actually said, "Wait a minute, this prevailing thought is entirely wrong." But close inspection is necessary to understand the depth of this denial of race. The truth is that an entire society goes out of its way to show or even prove Spanish descent while single-handedly leaving out African heritage. One example of the lengths to which people go to control their image is the dictator Rafael Trujillo, El Benefactor, who would regularly use whitening creams or powders and coerced writers to embellish his European roots. He even created his own brand: Presidential Powder. (If you were to visit a Dominican pharmacy today, you would still find skin-lightening creams for sale, with celebrities and athletes like Sammy Sosa as paid endorsers.) Apparently, Trujillo's greatest frustration was that he was not fully accepted in the highest tier of society because his father's mother was Haitian.
>
> Conversations with Dominicans about family roots jump quickly to Spanish ascendance. "My grandfather was the son of Spaniards" is a commonly heard expression of pride. It is as though Dominicans feel that being Spanish is a better pedigree than being of African descent. In many parts of the world, including the Dominican Republic, admitting that you have African roots is admitting far more than just heritage. It is admitting that you have struggled. It is admitting that your forefathers may have been slaves. It is admitting that your skin color may have landed you worse jobs. It is admitting that you may feel less valued than others who are whiter. This is the reality of Dominican society when it comes to color. Family members might even advise, "Being white is a career in itself here, so be careful who you marry." Black is not beautiful to many Dominicans. So if you are indeed black, you want to excuse

your way out of it, and you want to straighten your hair, and you want to look and feel and be whiter.

This denial seems shameful at first glance. What is the big deal? What is life like if you are white in the Dominican Republic? Would you be surprised to find out that the wealthiest Dominicans are white? Would you be surprised to find out that most business owners and managers are lighter skinned? Take a walk into the country clubs, the elite social groupings, the top corporate meetings, and count heads. You will see a dominant white society in control and still suppressing the darker-skinned ones. Some black people are evident, but the higher you climb socially, the lighter it all gets.

Take a look at the history of the Dominican Republic, and you will have a pretty close telling of what still is. We do have to take the term "white" relatively here—lightly, if you will. Because people have mixed interracially, you can find a lot of people of color calling darker people black. From a distance, this seems odd, since most of the people around here would be classified as black in other parts of the world.

In fact, so strong is Dominicans' effort to deny being black that terms like *Indio oscuro* ("dark Indian") are used instead. This is a social compromise for saying you have some color, but not enough to be flat-out black. The government even goes to great lengths to differentiate two categories on drivers' licenses: *trigueño* (dark with curly hair) and *mestizo* (dark with straight hair). Even legally, your Dominican documents might describe you as white just because you lack evident African features. If your nose is considered fine, your skin lighter, or your face Hispanic-looking or having European features, you pass for white. "Black" is being African-looking with very stereotypical features. This also leads to a large amount of the mixed population defaulting to "white" and not "black."

Continuing through the museum, artworks are organized by era, with the fall of Rafael Trujillo, an admirer of Adolf Hitler who wore a similar moustache, marking a divide. Work created during the reign of El Jefe, who was referred to as "the chief, the stick, and the Constitution," is without conscience—there are no social issues or raw emotions portrayed. The work inspired after his fall in 1961 screams of anger and injustice, of a time when people felt it was finally safe to reclaim their cities.

Also in Santiago, not far from the León museum, is the Tomás Morel Folkloric Museum, which most people drive by unknowingly without appreciating the beauty inside. The most prominent features of this museum, aside from the endearing couple who run it, are the hundreds of vibrant, authentic Carnival masks on display. Each February, Dominicans observe Carnival (translated as "farewell to flesh"), which began as a celebration of their independence from Spain and is still seen as a joyful reinforcement of their identity. Professionals and amateurs alike make new masks each year in hopes of winning one of the top prizes. Many artists conceal their creations until the first day of the event for surprise value. The highlight of the festival is a parade containing characters such as the Limping Devil, the Bear Man, the Indian, and the Chicken Robber. The masks, some of which incorporate real teeth and bull horns, are said to spiritually change the people wearing them. If you are able to attend, be cautious of participants carrying what look like balloons on sticks, which are actually inflated cow stomachs used to smack passersby.

Our drive between the two museums took us past the monument to the three Mirabal sisters who were killed in 1960 for rebelling during Trujillo's reign. Their deaths inspired the United Nations to establish the International Day for the Elimination of Violence against Women, held every year on November 25, the day of their slaying. Their story is best captured in Julia Alvarez's novel *In the Time of the Butterflies*, which focuses on the game Trujillo made of not letting one of the sisters pursue her dream of becoming the first female lawyer in the Dominican Republic. Seeing their memorial while scanning the Santiago streets, with children playing *trompo* (a game where you spin a table leg by tying a rope around it), threw me into a flashback.

Las hermanas' story unfolded vividly before us a few years ago when Kevin arranged a once-in-a-lifetime chat with the surviving sister, whose current home was the sisters' first. Never in my life had I felt like I had encountered history as I did on that day. As a warm-up to the main event, we visited Salcedo, where the sisters' last home is now a museum.

It takes about an hour to drive east from Santiago to Salcedo, which is located in the bountiful Cibao Valley. It's easy to tell when you are nearing their home because of the countless butterfly murals—on the amphitheater, on the water tower, on the stores. When you enter the rustic yet elegant home—yellow and brown, with open wooden windows—where they lived out their last ten months, it seems as if the women might return at any minute to pick up their busy lives. The dinner table is neatly set for eight, school-made embroideries decorate the home, wedding photos hang in the hallway, and their closets are full. Our tour guide also pointed out Patria's elegant teacup collection, Minerva's typewriter with controversial thesis and 14th of June Movement flag nearby, and a braid of Maria Teresa's hair. An even more intimate display, set on a pedestal, contains the belongings recovered with the sisters' bodies: three purses, a shoe, some jewelry, and a bloodied handkerchief used to clean the bodies. Trujillo always referred to them as personal, not political, enemies.

From there we went to meet the living legend, Dedé Mirabal, at her home. Fortunately, I had taken Kevin's advice to read Alvarez's novel before the trip, so I had some background on Las Mariposas. We sat on her spacious porch for over an hour, each teacher on the edge of his chair, each teacher changed forever.

Dedé's home is a spacious one-story marvel with a robust garden. Fittingly, countless butterflies have made their home in this haven and occasionally fluttered onto the porch, which left us catching our breath. Dedé herself is a petite woman with amazing fortitude. She was very welcoming and wouldn't sit until each of us had a comfortable place. Then she settled into a chair with our interpreter and Kevin to her right. Dedé, with her dark hair and silver streak, was wearing an intricate butterfly brooch. Kevin wore an expression of great anticipation.

Once everyone was situated and had had their fill of the fresh atmosphere, Kevin explained to Dedé our purpose on the island and said that most of us had read the famous book and that if she was comfortable with it, we would enjoy hearing what life was like for her and her family back in the 1950s. Dedé nodded as the interpreter translated and then became still. For a moment, she looked off into the distance, seemingly collecting herself. Then she smiled slightly and began by telling us that her childhood had been a very happy one. From there, she weaved an amazing tale of love, risk, and rebellion, as if she were reliving the moments there with us. She spoke about when her dad, a farmer, was imprisoned and declared a Communist to intimidate the sisters. Dedé noted that she had never been active in the underground movement, and that that was why she wasn't murdered, but she spoke about the uniqueness of a mostly male force led foremost by her sister Minerva. After her sisters were killed, she said, she took on the responsibility of caring for their six children.

Dedé took us higher and higher, each tale more exciting than the last. Then somberness set in when she spoke of that rainy November day when her sisters were ambushed, dragged out of their vehicle, brutally beaten, shot, placed back in their vehicle, and pushed into a ravine. (When I was taken to the spot where the murders took place, on the mountains between Puerto Plata and Santiago [on the sisters way back from visiting their imprisoned husbands], the driver had to navigate around the remains of burnt tires from a recent protest over the poor conditions of the street, which she nicknamed "nightmare road.")

Dedé gestured frequently and passionately as she told the story. Our teachers were teary-eyed within minutes. It was as if she had conjured the spirits of her sisters, and they were there with us. Every once in a while we would look at one another to reassure ourselves that this was really happening. The energy was overwhelming as Dedé took us deeper and deeper into the days when people looked over their shoulders as they spoke.

Dedé said her mother was coerced, in order to protect the remaining members of her family, into signing a document stating that the deaths of her three daughters and the staged crash had been an accident. Added to that was the pain of having the murderer constantly watching over the survivors, because the penalty for not hanging portraits of Trujillo in the home was having your fingers cut off—perhaps a homage to the policies under Columbus's rule on the island.

After more than an hour, which left us all drained of emotion, Dedé finished her story by saying, "My sisters were martyrs." Then she stopped suddenly, as if a trance had been lifted. The momentary silence was broken by one word: *"¿Preguntas?"* (Questions?) We didn't hesitate. After a while, a young lady came onto the porch and said we needed to wrap things up. We applauded Dedé, and she hugged us as we left. I was able to take an amazing photo of her with my principal and a former student that Kevin now includes on his poster boards highlighting the tours. We got on the bus and were off. Across from Dedé's home, we passed the mangled frame of a jeep—what was salvaged from the wreckage of the staged accident.

George Santos's parents offered two points of view on Trujillo:

It has been fifty-one years since the assassination of the tyrant Rafael Leonidas Trujillo Molina[40], a figure who governed with a very strong hand over thirty years in the Dominican Republic. His government started in 1930, and a few months later a hurricane called San Zenon completely destroyed the capital city of Santo Domingo, leaving very few buildings unharmed, those made of concrete. That disaster gave Trujillo the opportunity to completely rebuild the city. He baptized it with the name Trujillo City.

The renaming of the capital marked the beginning of the regime that, initially aided by the American government, restructured the police, the armed forces, and the general administration of the country, maintaining sustainable development until the hour of his death. Back then, the city and the towns looked impeccably clean. Citizens would be fined if they would dare toss trash out on the streets. The patriotic symbols were ever-present and highly respected. Human sanity and environmental principles were the regime's fundamental philosophy.

Trujillo freed the country of millions in foreign debt and opened industries of all sorts that provided jobs to a very significant number of citizens. Factories quickly dominated the landscape: for shoes, weapons, cold cuts, bread, crackers, and dairy from the finest quality of cattle that could be found. In a nutshell, he motorized the economy of the country on many levels of life for Dominicans. Everything I have mentioned so far was done within a frame of absolute control of the political life of every Dominican. Books were not allowed that had any sort of revolutionary ideas. You were not allowed to listen to radio stations from countries having anything to do with Communism. You were expected to love the tyrant, and you needed to be in absolute agreement with the regime so you could live within a certain guaranteed tranquility.

It is common nowadays, sadly, to think of going back to an era when we were under tyranny because of the current lack of authority, of environmental sanity, institutional organization, and

---

[40] After Trujillo's assassination, Dominicans celebrated by singing "They killed the Goat in the street."

respect for any sort of order. Everything in life has a good side, and tyrannies have a horribly bad side, with a tragic toll of murders and disappearances of valuable human lives that no one can ever forget.

Julia Sánchez, Santo Domingo—2012

I grew up in Mao and Santo Domingo, with my entire childhood as Trujillo being the dictator. The order that was experienced in the cities and the government institutions was at too high a cost. I believe that freedom should be in the hands of the people and should be above everything else in a country. If we are deprived of that, everything else makes no sense and lacks value. I still remember how it used to be obligatory in every home in the Dominican Republic to hang an 8-by-20 picture of Trujillo that read below, "In this home, Trujillo is the boss." The press was absolutely controlled by the dictatorship as well. It was a regime of terror.

The nation was very quickly terrorized by the military. Support for the dictatorship was obligatory, but I wouldn't call it universal support. There was a strong military pressure with oppressive forces protecting the regime. There was also a team of informants, called the *caliés*, who quickly reported any sign of insubordination or disagreements, which would bring down immediate and sometimes fatal consequences. They belonged to a group called the SIM (Military Intelligence Service), and you could see them driving around in black Volkswagen buggies. If they passed by your home several times, you were in deep trouble. There were centers of interrogation, where torture was an everyday thing, called "The Forty" and "The Nine." They were two of the most terrible places known in the history of the dictatorship. "The Forty" was outside of the city and counted Minerva and Maria Teresa Mirabal among its prisoners, and "The Nine" was on the ninth kilometer toward the San Isidro Air Base.

Every important business in the Dominican Republic had to be influenced by Trujillo and his family. Owners of competitive businesses were labeled enemies of the state and imprisoned. There was no economic freedom. This led to Trujillo becoming the second richest person in Latin America. The dictator or an immediate family member was converted into the owner of every major corporation nationwide. The great business families of the Dominican Republic, stockholders, and CEOs had to be in direct association with the dictator's family.

The Catholic Church did not oppose a phrase that was institutionalized in most parts of the nation and made public: *Dios y Trujillo* ("God and Trujillo"). The Catholic Church also made collective baptisms where the dictator became the godfather of scores of children. Many of them would later on be called Rafael in his honor. I was born to a family that was mistreated during Trujillo's era. Trujillo wanted to "take" one of the daughters of my great uncle. My grandfather's brother was absolutely opposed to this and looked to send her to Mexico so he could hide her there. This act of defiance would cost him dearly. The permission to leave the country had to be granted by the dictator himself, which it was in this case. Later on it became evident why the permission was actually requested, and my grandfather's brother was shot and killed on his own farmland.

Trujillo was a megalomaniac, but he was not crazy. I would never say he was crazy. His actions were premeditated, and insanity doesn't allow for that. On the other hand, those who were favored were favored well. I can recall my wife's uncle, Miguel Angel Vega, who was a pharmacist who also had an arms store allowed by Trujillo. In fact, there were only three entities who were allowed to sell arms during his reign: the Vega family in the North, the Read Warehouse, and Olivo's Armory (which belonged to a general of Trujillo's).

In my opinion, Trujillo was the product and the legacy of the occupation by the North Americans from 1916 to 1924. It was during that time that Trujillo entered the army—the very army created by the Americans. When the USA left in 1924, Trujillo was already a high-ranking officer. By 1930 he assumed power by overthrowing President Horacio Vásquez. America's support of Trujillo's dictatorship began to decline when an attempt to assassinate Rómulo Betancourt, the president of Venezuela, in 1960 proved threatening to US interests. The American administration then started to see evidence for the need to discontinue support of Trujillo and eventually put an end to the dictatorship. In 1961,

Trujillo was assassinated with help from his very close, high-ranking officers and with assistance from the CIA.

In essence, the lack of so many fundamental freedoms to me has no justification. The end of the dictatorship was necessary so the Dominican Republic could start cementing its democracy.

Jose Santos, Santo Domingo—2012

Our farewell night

Chapter 10
WITH CHARITY, THE GIVING HAND IS STILL ON TOP

A Dios rogando, y con el mazo dando.
(To God begging and with the stick beating.)

As you might guess, the place I reflect on most when I am back in the States is the batey. After walking hand-in-hand with a youth whose destiny seems all but sealed, you are forever changed. It has the power to build or break your spirit. While one colleague referred to it as hell on earth, I think of it as the ultimate Rorschach test—how you take it in reveals your character. The batey, like all the places we visited during that week, led to deep discoveries. There is no other place I have ever been that reveals so many truths—about life, about human nature, and about myself.

The most intriguing part of visiting these shantytowns was the locals' hospitality—plucking fruit off trees for us and slicing it open with a machete, finding plastic chairs for our comfort, and plopping babies in our laps. A common revelation overheard during the trip is, "They are giving *us* charity." One teacher who had been on the trip multiple times said, "That's the one thing I want everybody to understand about bateys—how the people, especially the kids, are always filled with joy." The one thing that hasn't been destroyed yet in the bateys is their sense of community. Forcing people to live in meager conditions has one side effect governments and corporations seem to overlook: solidarity. Efforts to tear them apart just bring them closer together.

On a teacher tour a couple of years back, over some fine dining in Santo Domingo's Colonial Zone after a visit to a batey, a few people voiced disappointment that they hadn't brought more for the impoverished people they had just befriended. Not being able to hold my tongue that night—the heat was probably a factor—I said sarcastically, "I'm pretty sure they will be there again tomorrow, and most likely they'll still be poor." And I didn't end my outburst there; damn that sweltering heat. "We could simply take up a collection right now, and I am certain Rich will make sure they receive it and share it evenly." (It's times like these when I wonder if I'm more of an asset or a liability on Kevin's trips.) At that point, I offered my pinky to a *greñua* (crazy-haired woman) giving me an evil look, in the traditional Dominican "swear of enemies," which seemed to fluster her. Rich, who seemed to know exactly where I was going, nodded toward the entire table and said, "I'll actually be back there in three days."

I would like to say pesos of many colors started to fly out of people's wallets. I'd also like to say world leaders got together last weekend, realized there's more than enough food to feed everybody, and decided to work together to end hunger. Would you like to guess how many people at our table dug out even one peso after they were informed that, at that moment, they could alleviate their feelings of frustration for not having been able to give more?

When I speak with likeminded people about charity, it's amazing how many use words like "guilt" and "selfishness" in their articulate responses about people's motivation to help others. Many of my friends believe that, as a common symptom of "affluenza," people donate money to feel absolved. Could that be the reason so many gave after the 2010 earthquake in Haiti—that they felt guilty about not having done anything earlier? And why do we give more during geological catastrophes than during genocides and wars? Is it that acts of nature have obvious victims? Perhaps it is because natural disasters are closer to home—"it can happen to anyone at any time"—and thus more relatable than corrupt governments, broken education systems, or structural racism.

Aside from educators and students, I recommend Kevin's tour to psychology buffs. If you are a fan of behavior and reasoning, as I am, these social justice tours give you the most amazing insight into human nature. The juxtaposition of poverty and privilege leads to many revelations.

Over appetizers on the last night of that tour, half the table was in agreement that if they had known the level of poverty these people were living in, they would have brought more. "How could you not want to give more?" one teacher said despondently. Yet, five short minutes after this collective misery was announced, a practical solution was offered, and there were no takers. It just didn't make sense. Did they or didn't they want to help?

I guess what they say about the purest charity being done anonymously could have made for a deep discussion, or we could have weighed the notion that charity is no way to extend dignity and is therefore counterproductive. However, it was our last night, and there would be no more debriefings. Plus, I figured I had ruffled enough feathers for one day, and I never want people on the tour to have their memories of Kevin's trip clouded because of one of my tangents.

Another controversy popped up when a teacher claimed that a Peace Corps worker who had taken us to see his work site and his host family was a hypocrite after she overheard him say he was putting his experience in the Dominican Republic on his résumé. I couldn't fight the urge and facetiously blurted out, "That sneaky bastard!"[41]

So what have we learned? We are more willing to give in person because it feels good. We cannot list any humanitarian actions on our résumé because that crosses a line. Well, what about on our tax forms? Where does that fall on the continuum?

---

[41] This comment was made during a different trip. I allow myself one blowup per summer, or two when it has been a really hot week.

When it comes to helping those who struggle, I don't believe charity solves anything. We need to make a shift from charity to justice if we're going to have an impact. Lilla Watson summed up trips like Kevin's best: "If you have come to help me, you are wasting your time. But if you have come because your liberation is tied with mine, then let us work together." I believe we are all connected—spiritually, yes, but more so when it comes to our lifestyles. I get to live comfortably because others do not. My clothes and electronics are easy purchases because those making them in a free trade zone are not earning a living wage. The produce I buy at the supermarket is inexpensive because someone is harvesting it for less than a dollar an hour. It was Dr. Martin Luther King Jr. who wrote, "And before you finish eating breakfast in the morning, you've depended on more than half the world." My privilege is tied to others' poverty.

"Give a man a fish, and you feed him for a day. Teach a man to fish, and you feed him for a lifetime." I believe it is similar with charity. If I give a person twenty dollars, it will help him for a day, or a week, and I will feel good about myself for about as long. However, if I can somehow connect with him, understand his story, and take action in a meaningful way either on the island or at home, then I will have made the difference of a lifetime. Charity should never be a substitute for justice.

Having taken part in all twelve of Kevin's tours over seven years, I have built some amazing bonds on the island, and I can tell you that there is a powerful difference between the reception we receive now when we arrive at a batey, a sweatshop, or the garbage dump, and the reception we received our first time. On our early visits, the people were pleasant but seemed a bit weary. Now that Kevin is into double digits with the tours, we are showered with unconditional love and invitations to Vodou ceremonies. "Hugs and kisses for everybody" is something we hear frequently from our friends on the island when we return for another four weeks.

Have our visits made their situations better? Maybe. Foremost is the idea of knowing you are not alone. When you struggle, and nobody is there to walk with you, life can seem hopeless. But when you are in a rough spot and feel others are on your side, and in your corner, anything seems possible.

It is said that with charity, the giving hand is still on top. Kevin realized this early on and made it his mission to bring visitors to the island not for some heroic adventure, or for photo opportunities with the poor they had helped, just so they could go back to the States feeling better about themselves.[42] Instead, we play games, pick up trash, enjoy home-cooked meals, and hold hands while chatting on front porches. As teachers, we are in the memory-making business, and that is what the struggling people of the Dominican Republic need more than handouts—meaningful connections and support from outsiders.

Our last day on the island with the students was very emotional. Kevin looked proud and hopeful, wondering if the seeds planted on the trip would take root. Most of the students wore bittersweet smiles. It was clear many were considering scenarios that would allow them to extend their stay, while simultaneously yearning to return home and share their photographs and stories on Facebook to see how their friends would respond to their travels.

Kevin scheduled one last meeting in the morning because we had come home late after the previous night's bonfire with the DREAM (Dominican Republic Education and Mentoring) Project students. He wanted to offer them closure and make sure the students understood the threads connecting all our activities that week. Even though it seemed simple, one of the most memorable events of the teen tour was the scavenger hunt through the DREAM kids' community. One of the more popular Dominicans we worked with, an eleven-year-old named Roberto, had only been away from home for a few hours but still ran up to the porch to give his mom a big hug, right in front of his friends. I was admiring the family-first display while staring at a mother duck in the front yard keeping an eye on her babies, which were frolicking in a pool made from a tire sliced in half. When Roberto introduced me to his mother, I commented on how adorable the ducks were, and she asked if I would like one. Being family-oriented and generous is just part

---

[42] We advise participants on both tours that when taking photos of people they meet, aim for family-style photos like ones you would display at home, as opposed to pictures of them in less dignified contexts.

of the fiber of some people. For others who haven't reached that point, I like to take an "if you fold a paper in one direction enough times, a crease will eventually develop" approach.

DREAM is a nonprofit organization that believes education is one way to transform communities. It employs locals and uses an international volunteer program to get children off the streets and into schools. Since most students in the Dominican Republic only attend school for half days, DREAM offers supplemental classes in the morning and the afternoon so students can get in a full day of learning. In addition to academic courses, it offers enrichment classes such as guitar and yoga. The teen program offers the same options as the younger classes, plus three additional ones: HIV/AIDS prevention, workforce development (gaining work readiness skills), and documentation (getting students birth certificates).

At the group's site in Cabarete, Molly Hamm, DREAM's monitoring, evaluation, and learning coordinator, told us it wasn't enough just to change the school system; you have to go into homes. DREAM workers are very engaged in family outreach, offering parents simple strategies like having their children read aloud to them while they prepare meals. The organization also has a school library that is open to the public and a mobile library that travels to schools in hopes of "creating a culture of reading." When we visited the classrooms at the DREAM school, I noticed the posted mission:

> Our vision is that all children born in the Dominican Republic have the opportunity to receive an education and learn to their full potential. It is our hope that our efforts can be multiplied to allow the opportunity for every child's gifts and challenges to be met with support. It is our goal to break the cycle of poverty and change people's destinies. It is our dream that the world will be a better place for the children and families of the next generation.

With our luggage standing in the distance and the students sitting in a semicircle, Kevin concluded the social justice tour. "Today is not the day I leave, but the day I plan my return!" he said. (I guess he didn't think there were enough teary eyes already.) He spoke more about the future than the past and thanked the students profusely for taking a leap of faith with his tour. He seemed to be avoiding eye contact with his own two children, probably because he was afraid he would break down and not be able to finish his speech.

"During our week on the island, we moved from charity to justice," he said. "Now let's inform others about the big issues we saw firsthand: clean water, public education, discrimination." The best way to teach teens something is to empower them to teach it to others, and in the process they might become more active and responsible citizens. Kevin's final message was clear: pass it on!

My last message to the students began, "Aside from those of us here right now, you'll meet very few in your lifetime who have ever done anything close to what you accomplished this week." Looking directly at the high school juniors, I added, "Colleges are going to drool over your applications when you write about your experiences here." I then challenged all of them to keep in mind the question I had asked earlier in the week: What is poverty? I repeated two of their responses: "a lack of access to the things people need to have comfort" and "not having ways to solve your basic problems." None of their definitions mentioned money. One bold student then commented to a neighbor but not to the whole group, "I think we are impoverished."

Last-day feedback is something I always look forward to. That's when the big question is answered: What resonated with our students? Kevin continued the meeting by reminding us that "a powerful experience can be either a window or a mirror." The students' reactions gave the impression that their experiences had been both.

"They really are the same as us. The only difference is the opportunities." "Maybe we should be making our lives more like theirs." "If I came here on vacation, I wouldn't have seen any of these things." "I want to stop living my life passively." Another student recalled her thoughts before she decided to go on the trip: "After hearing Kevin speak at my university, I thought, 'A white guy bringing people to the DR . . . this should be fun!'"

The final meeting on the most recent teacher tour had a similarly enlightened tone. "You really think you know what poverty is, and then you meet these people, and it changes your whole definition." "Seeing people stand up for what they believe in has inspired me to take this energy back home." "People can find happiness under any conditions." "This trip has reminded me of what's really important in life and what I should be focusing on." "I liked the trip because it wasn't run from a *pobrecito* ('poor boy') perspective." "When I was raised, I was always reminded that I had Taíno blood but never told about my African roots. I will leave this trip questioning my own identity as a Dominican."

After the students shared their thoughts about the trip's impact and how they would bring the experiences back with them, we got together for one last group photo. When it was time to start loading the buses, I saw my Polish student, Brygida, wander uncertainly toward Kevin. She gave him a big hug. Because of the overwhelming emotions of the day, she was only able to muster one sentence, but it was one that he'll never forget: "Thank you for the greatest week of my life."

Just in case the students weren't leaving with enough last-day moments to reflect on, there was one final, unexpected reminder of how unique our eight days on the island had been, and that came from our bus driver, Geovanny. The former police officer and tour comedian with limited English, who had a surprisingly soft singing voice, may have been smiling on the last day, but several of the students spied the tears he sometimes lifted his shades to wipe away. And that was the icing on the *bizcocho*.

While we were at the airport getting ready to send the students and parents off, the mood was tense. Kevin and I didn't take the flight back with them because we had the teachers' tour around the corner. The parents were fine with this arrangement because our interpreter, a fellow teacher in our school district, would be flying with the students. Oddly, once a bird decided to do its business on Alexa's travel forms, the atmosphere lightened. Perhaps it was a little payback for her giving Kevin and me a scare on the flight over.

In addition to having the week of their lives, many of the teens who have taken part in Kevin's social justice tour are off doing amazing things: receiving a scholarship to Harvard University, signing up for tours of duty with the Peace Corps, working as a camp counselor for the DREAM students, committing to international law as a college major. But you wouldn't know about these incredible feats by chatting with Kevin. That is what's amazing about Kevin—it's never about him. He doesn't jump in front of the camera, brag about the once-in-a-lifetime moments on the trip, or run off to newspapers with stories about the group's latest adventures. During the most recent teacher tour, I literally had to push Kevin in front of the television camera when they were looking for our reactions right after we met with leaders of the Dominican Republic's national teachers' union. That is why I have taken it upon myself to toot his horn and tell you the stories you wouldn't otherwise hear. That is why this book had to be written.

People often ask how Kevin's project is received in our middle school. Kevin, like myself, gets along very well with 90 percent of the faculty. As for the other 10 percent—to whom I refer, despite the math, as the 1 percent—they openly harbor a "we should help our own before we help outsiders" mind-set. The letters they send to our administration from time to time are unsigned, but we know who they are because a few cannot hold back their frustrations and jealousies. It's not that there are a lot of them, but more of a "those who know the least know it the loudest" situation. Countless times, I have overheard their three favorite terms when describing their issues with Kevin's approach: "empowers," "indoctrinates," and "makes them feel entitled." Some of the more brazen in the group have done things like take down Kevin's multicultural display boards seconds after he put them up in the teachers' cafeteria, *while he was still in the room*; tear up a playbill he created when the local high school's Haitian Club came to our school to perform and then stuff it in his mailbox; and, in the case of one teacher, go to great lengths to release noxious fumes whenever he passed Kevin alone in the hallway—a tactic I can only assume he learned while watching *Animal Planet*.

One incident I witnessed firsthand happened after Kevin released an issue of the student newspaper and left copies around the school. Not surprisingly, the altercation went down in the teachers' cafeteria, that breeding ground of hostility. The cover story featured an article on immigration written by a Haitian student. "It's not immigration, it's an invasion!" a teacher blurted out as she picked up the paper and threw it back down—a phrase likely borrowed from Fox News. The room, including more than one foreign-born teacher, went silent. Five seconds went by before I decided to shatter that silence. "Anyone who knows anything about the history of our country knows that we are a nation of immigrants," I said. "During every century since we became a free nation, we have experienced sporadic waves of immigration, and side by side with those masses of desperate people were those who felt the need to put them down just because they seemed different." She gave no counter response, so I returned to my lunch. Several minutes later, I went to leave the room, and that teacher and two colleagues were whispering right outside the door. Upon seeing me, they hesitated and then, without a word, scattered.

As for how their group finally fell apart, it's a funny story. Our principal, and then the superintendent, went on Kevin's tour. All of a sudden, the group seemed to catch a bad case of laryngitis.

Whenever Kevin introduces the trip to potential participants or discusses the Dominican Republic with someone for the first time, he always mentions the same starting point: Christopher Columbus. When people ask for my perspective on the trip, I, too, reference Columbus. I like to classify tourists into two categories: those with a Columbus mentality and those who are more open-minded.

"If only they had more education or worked harder" is the song people with the Columbus mentality sing. They have a "lazy natives" mind-set. "If they only grabbed a book once in a while, instead of dominos, they wouldn't be in this mess." So much for not blaming the victim.

On one tour, a parent stuck resolutely to his summation of the issues. He would knock on a nearby surface and ask the students what that noise was. "That's the sound of opportunity knocking! Can you hear it?" I found his choice of words interesting because he used the term that most participants find conspicuously missing on the trip: opportunity. People tend to go with the simplest explanation their minds can conjure, conveniently dismissing their own part in the equation. I argue that the poverty in the Dominican Republic is more about a lack of resources and opportunities than a lack of work ethic, but it typically falls on deaf ears.

Then there's the gray area—people who say they cannot go on a tour like Kevin's because it will force them to take action. "If I go," they say, "then I'll have to do something about it."

To which I offer: ships are safest when in harbor, but that's not why they were built.

So is the Dominican Republic the second-happiest place on earth, as CNN recently reported? Before my first trip, I expected to see misery everywhere, but it was only back in the States that I recognized widespread depression and desperation. I guess I have come full circle: this place is going to be beautiful—this place is going to be miserable—this place indeed holds pure beauty and true happiness. Kevin, who feels that his truth is still developing, seems to have gone through his own evolution: the Dominican Republic is a developing country—the Dominican Republic has lots of wealth and natural resources, but they are extracted in ways that contaminate the environment, and the people are not paid fairly—the poverty in the Dominican Republic is not natural but man-made, built on a history of injustice.

When strangers ask about the trip, they assume we are going there to build homes or schools. "No, we are going to learn from the people about their struggles, and to extend our solidarity," Kevin says. He then tries to explain that you cannot go to the Dominican Republic to build a house for those who need it most because people in the bateys live as squatters. Because they don't own the land, building a house doesn't necessarily create stability for them. "We're going there not to grab hammers but to learn," he says. "There are many complex questions underlying the roots of extreme poverty. There are no easy answers, but the experience might at least undo stereotypes and complicate their way of thinking about poverty both at home and abroad."

Right before sending this book to press, I felt it was the appropriate time to ask Kevin one final question: what have you learned from all your experiences in the Dominican Republic? He responded, "If you go to a developing country to build homes, you are a hero. If you go and start asking questions, you are a troublemaker."

George Santos's final thoughts:

When thinking about the Dominican Republic, I am struck by one fact. Most people appear to be in some way or another happy, and at worst content with what they have. There is a general lax attitude that resembles the innocence of the unsuspecting indigenous who once called this land home. Why is this? Why isn't anything really a big deal to Dominicans? Why is it that hardly anyone has a chip on his shoulder? What's with this lack of urgency, this "*mañana* mentality"?

We are a nation of "no problem." Culturally, we have low self-esteem. We don't fight for our rights. We think, why make a big deal over this? We don't go around suing one another.

The truth is, no one can answer this question with precision, but I believe there are factors pointing us in the right direction. Three factors, to be exact: the first being the generosity and fertility of the land. The northern valleys of the Dominican Republic, particularly the Cibao Valley, are some of the most fertile lands in the Caribbean. Crops that have the privilege to feast on its soil and drink from its water are robust, healthy, bright green, plentiful, and well nourished.

The second factor is the lack of seasonal deadly weather. In the Dominican Republic, you don't need to work hard to be ready for a harsh winter. At this latitude, between the Tropic of Cancer and the equator, you just don't do that. No matter how little you prepare, the climate will not punish you with death, aside from the hurricanes that can cause some serious damage. The reality here is that, year to year, very little preparation will not really hurt you.

Lastly, and thankfully, there is also a lack of famine. This land has not starved a population to death. It is still so pristine and fertile that its people can enjoy crops all year long, facing tough times occasionally like too much or too little rain, but historically there are no records of massive famine. Just pick a fruit somewhere, and you eat. The land is so generous, fruits can be found in just about any corner at any time of the year.

These three factors may contribute to that lack of a rush to get something done. It is geographic wealth in a mostly poor setting.

I remember thanking the members of Kevin's group for being given the privilege of coguiding them along the beaches, curves of land, and hilltops that paint this island. Why was I feeling so thankful? The reason fell somewhere between Pedro Mir's poem "Hay un pais en el mundo" ("There Is a Country in the World"), which speaks of a place "wild and uninhabited," "of sugar and alcohol," "abused and kicked," and my own love for this place and its people. You see, for as long as I can remember, I have witnessed many visitors come here to take something from her, from Hispaniola. Taking a shell, a lover, drunken memories, its food, its fresh air and virgin beaches, its innocence, anything its people offer out of kindness or need. Yet this bunch of travelers came to take nothing from her. They came to ask her name, what she likes, to dance and sing with her, and to admire her beauty—her majestic, mesmerizing, breathtaking beauty. These friends came to ask about her troubles. I watched them ask her name, and what makes her eyes shine. It felt as if, for the first time in a very long time, she was being treated with the dignity and respect that she deserves. Like a lady, Hispaniola smiled at these rare visitors. And if she could speak, she probably would have said, "Thank you. This is who I really am."

Ramonsito's Vodou workshop

Epilogue

A student of mine once said, "Books take you places when you can't get there on foot." For those who haven't been to the DR or experienced extreme poverty up close, I hope this book served its purpose.

The content in this book has been fact-checked many times by several people. If it is the case that something slipped our notice, please contact me, and I will make the adjustment in a future edition of the book.

Lastly, I would like to thank you, the reader, for giving *The Dominican Experiment* a chance. I hope I didn't disappoint, and I hope you wind up taking the official "Page 81 Challenge." My time on the island has become a wondrous chapter in my life, and I plan on visiting the island many more times, as it has made me who I am. Who knows, perhaps one day we'll board the same bus, and you'll get a bear hug from Rich, a juicy nugget of knowledge from George, or watch Kevin, "The Hulk," tear another shirt.